T0290557

# TRIDENT
# A
# TRADING
# STRATEGY

BY CHARLES L. LINDSAY

WINDSOR BOOKS

WINDSOR BOOKS
P.O. Box
Brightwaters, NY



ISBN 978-0-930233-48-8

Library of Congress Catalog Card Number 76-27500
PRINTED IN THE UNITED STATES OF AMERICA

*Dedication*

*This book is dedicated to the few serious Commodity Price-Action Researchers who spend countless hours pursuing the rhyme and reason of market action. The search for practical Truth in the chaos of market action is truly a Labor of Love. Yet the truth does exist, and with its discovery, surely public trading in Commodities will be outlawed forever . . .*

*I wish to express sincere appreciation to the many Trident Students and friends throughout the United States and Canada whose inspiration and enthusiasm made this book a reality . . .*

*Charles L. Lindsay*

# CONTENTS

# THE STORY OF TRIDENT

# CHAPTER 1

Telling the Trident story is a joy and relived experience because it is a story of impressions and a chronology of significantly remembered events. Time has mellowed memory to the extent that many of the events are quite humorous now, but were very frustrating during the time they occurred. To relive the Trident story is akin to visiting an old friend. The opportunity to participate in the reconstruction of the highlights brings back sufficient memories to know that the experience was not only worthwhile but incredibly significant.

***6:45 p.m. Friday July 6th, 1973***

The gnawing uneasiness in the pit of the stomach did not pass, though the dinner was deliciously filling and the decision to water the newly seeded back yard was in retaliation to the mental haunt from the day's market action. To know commodities, and not know enough to win, was an ego blow for which there was no defense.

Without specific thoughts, yet somehow aware that the hose moved like it had a mind of its own. The pressure of the hose made a waving pattern as it produced fine water spray through the nozzle. Up and down, serpentine, somewhat like the price changes which had occurred that morning in the Commodity Market. The hose moving up and down, the market moving up and down, the hose, the market, the market, the hose, WOW!

It was clear that the water pressure forced through the nozzle of the hose, created continuous swings as water pressure built up and was then released. Each swing could be measured and therefore predicted or calculated. Certainly, there were mathematics which would express the pressure functions, even if some independent research would be required. The research should be done no matter how complicated. Thoughts flowed with clarity and rapidity while standing alone during that part of the day's end, just before sunset.

That day's uneasy feeling had been replaced with enthusiasm and an eagerness to sit in the light with pencil and paper, to explore all of the possibilities of independent price action, with a view towards predictability. That evening and into the next morning, numerical exploration did not cease nor did the enthusiasm wane. The overwhelming conclusion was that there existed a predictable point on each swing from which the price would move just as much above as below.

### *7:18 a.m. Monday July 9th, 1973*

The Broker was a medium sized man in his late forties or early fifties, with a manner which bespoke of a time he had been a high ranking Office Manager and Vice President of the firm. It was never known what had knocked him from his high perch. He was always willing to give advice, although it amounted to little more than a dissertation of why the price might go either way.

The broker was given an order: "Buy 2 Mar Sugar at 8.70 put a stop at 8.50." Above the normal buzz and hum of machines, stock quotation boards and the persistent random tick of the Commodity Board, the broker described a previous customer's order selling

Sugar at 8.70; clearly, one trader would make money, while the other trader would leave with that familiar uneasy feeling in his stomach. The new analysis researched over the weekend had indicated that on any given day the price of a specific commodity would rise just as high above a common trade point as it would fall below the same common point, and the calculated common trade point for Sugar was 8.70.

The thoughts were much lighter. The higher the price Sugar reached, the more in harmony all became. The new hypothesis was established; on any given day, a commodity could be bought or sold at the common trade point and at some point in time that day, the trade would make a profit. (The hose, the market, the market, the hose!) Content and enthusiastic, the sunset thought was reinforced by the rising price of Sugar, which by then was at 8.80. Even the Office Manager, whose head was magnificently bald, spoke that morning, (something he never did) seeming to reaffirm that all was well.

Without perceptible awareness, as thoughts of additional price action research passed at a near subconscious level, the price of Sugar ticked lower and lower and finally stood at the 8.70 mark again. Deeply aware that the price of Sugar was merely doing what had been predicted, a fact greatly appreciated, an even deeper awareness came through with startling clarity; the profit had disappeared and was turning into a loss.

"Sell 2 Mar Sugar at the market and hurry," the broker was instructed. With about seven minutes of trading time remaining that day, the Market Order was filled at 8.67 at a loss of $67.20. The sounds, faces and machines, so friendly and pleasantly harmonious, were now mildly irritating and less friendly. In the rush to leave for home, the broker was saying that the other client who sold Sugar that morning ended up with an identical loss of $67.20. The broker said something about the other client buying back at the close of the market and being filled at 8.73. The incredible paradox was that two clients with the same broker at approximately the same time, traded in opposite directions and both lost the same amount of money. The results proved something, but much research would be required before common trade point analysis would lead to reliable profit. Needless to say, the rest was uneasy that night, and for several nights during the next few days.

### *7:15 a.m. Thursday July 12th, 1973*

The data provided by the broker was more reliable than the research effort mounted thus far. The unique problem had been the fact that the trading strategy could not be that simple. It would be better to have a trading strategy that was sophisticated, dazzling, and somewhat mysterious, since the Commission House regulars would not respect anything as simple as: "buy a higher opening, sell a lower opening." The situation was reminiscent of a lingering definition of the word "sophistication as something simple made complicated." The specific investigation, which had been underway for the last several days, was whether or not a higher or lower market opening for a specific commodity led to predictability relative to the price of that commodity during the session.

The data; daily highs, lows, open, and close statistics, reflected price action in Silver, Copper, Wheat, Sugar, and Cattle. Startling, yet somewhat trivial, was the discovery that, in the case of Silver, 86% of the time a higher opening produced a price higher than the opening price by at least $100 or more. The other commodities researched produced a similar result at least 70% of the time or better. Commodity trading could not be that simple. It could not be, for every commodity trader would simply look for a higher opening to buy, and wait to grab the hundred-dollar-profit and run. A trading strategy merely based upon opening prices being higher or lower could not represent the fruits of what had become several hundred hours of active research. But, the statistical probabilities could not be ignored and therefore future trading would have to consider opening prices as a criteria.

So the strategy was set; buy the higher opening, wait for at least a $100 move and take the profit. The thought did occur, however, that in order to effect such a strategy, provision would have to be made for how much loss should be endured before the $100 profit was available At the time, the thought provided a basis for serious terror, especially considering the limited capital available for the strategy. Obviously additional refinement would be necessary before implementing such a plan in the real market.

Each market was watched with interest as it opened, but no trades were taken. As it turned out, the strategy was not particularly bad. The markets which opened higher, did in fact move higher on the day; those that opened lower, did move lower. However, in the case of two commodities which opened higher, the opening price remained the high of the day, as both markets proceeded promptly down the daily limit. The market opening strategy will always be remembered as something worthy of Mickey Mouse and perhaps a shade less.

***2:30 p.m. Friday July 13th, 1973***

The small Cocktail Lounge just off the lake was as good a place as any to mull over the day's market action. There were all of three people in the bar, but the young bartender was well known and quite a conversationalist. The one-sided conversation, about fantastic profits available in the Commodity Market, left him somewhat bewildered and unable to genuinely respond in his usual, jovial manner. The conversation continued in spite of the bartender's inability to appreciate the delicate intricacies of the emotional environment of the Commodity Market. That which seemed to fall on deaf ears was overheard with interest by those who privately eavesdrop.

He was in his mid-thirties, managed a nearby Service Station and drank beer. At an appropriate moment he eased into the conversation by saying, "a good friend has been encouraging me to get into the Commodity Market," Upon reflection it would have been better had his friend kept his mouth shut. His statement was sufficient to divert the conversation away from the bartender, freeing him to do things like cleaning glasses and wiping the bar, which he proceed to do with great gusto.

He was told about several commission house regulars, one of whom made $20,000 in Cattle that day, but could have walked away with $65,000 had he taken profit earlier; and the other who had grabbed $2,200 in Soybean Oil in about five minutes. The story about the two traders dwarfed the $320 profit experienced personally in Soybean Oil that day, but he was told about it anyway. It was obvious that he was trying to control the thought of quick and easy money, but he could not disguise the wide-eyed look of excitement and astonishment.

He wrote down the exact address of the Brokerage House, including the time Soybean Oil opened for trading. He refused the offer for a ride to the Brokerage House, but indicated he'd be there for sure. With that he left and the bartender was told to pour another Harvey Wallbanger. The thought that the Service Station Manager probably would never be seen again mixed well with the orange juice, Galliano and Vodka.

### *7:20 a.m. Monday July 16, 1973*

The Service Station Manager appeared at the Brokerage House just as he said he would. He wore a sheepish grin as he sat down in the next seat, saying nothing, and taking in all the sights, sounds, and personalities of those present. After a few moments he asked who he would have to see in order to establish a trading account. The broker was genuinely delighted to establish a new account and no doubt saw great promise in a novice who had no choice but to take his ambivalent advice.

It was not surprising that he mentioned he had entered an order to buy Soybean Oil. Soybean Oil opened moderately lower that morning, a fact which technically indicated selling on the day. He had high hopes of making a fast profit, and it would have been a crime to dash those hopes by sharing the newly researched market opening strategy with him. He seemed more pleased with the excitement of being involved rather than concerned that the price of Soybean Oil was swinging lower and lower.

He sat quietly watching each Soybean tick, getting excited whenever the price rallied. But the excitement passed quickly when the price dipped again. The acutely emotional experience was well known because it had happened many times before.

Towards the end of the trading session and without any warning, the Service Station Manager jumped straight up from his seat, babbled incoherently, saying "I've had enough of this, that's it, I've got to get out of this thing." By that time the price of Soybean Oil was fluctuating between down limit to nearly down limit and he was locked in with a loss of about $840. What he apparently felt was familiar to all. There was nothing that could be done other than have the broker go through the motions of rushing through an order to offset the trade. And that's exactly what the broker did. The other regular traders who knew of the situation, felt the situation regrettable, but managed to avoid expressing any sympathy. It was obvious that all present were acting as though they were walking on egg shells.

He staggered back to his seat, gathered up the few things that he had, glassy-eyed and in an apparent state of shock. He was observed by some of the traders to have bumped into a woman client, spun around twice, bumped into the glass exit door, mumbling "excuse me" several times to both the woman and the door along with other words too faint to hear. He was never seen or heard from again by anyone.

***10:15 a.m. Wednesday July 18th, 1973***

He was a tall, thin man, in his early sixties, who, with thick horned rimmed glasses, blended well with the familiar sights and sounds of the Brokerage House. He was the kind of person who had been part of the scenery for many years. Those who did not know him thought he was one of the Brokers, but he was actually a speculator. His specialty was day trading Silver. And, although he was never observed talking with other house speculators, he controlled specific territory in front of the constantly ticking Commodity Board.

That morning the broker said that the old guy up front had been trading Silver for as long as he could remember and maintained the same peculiar kinds of charts now known to the Broker as Swing Charts. The Broker felt that it might be mutually beneficial to sit down with the "old guy" and compare notes. The thought of approaching him to strike up a conversation was felt with mixed emotions because he had never been observed speaking to house regulars before.

He seemed to genuinely enjoy the conversation, as he was open, knowledgeable, and quite willing to share his daily Swing Charts which he prepared during each session of the market and refined through smoothing the following evening. He had promised to make copies of his current charts ready for the next day's trading. The remark which continues to echo in mind was the fact that, "no one else had ever bothered nor shown interest," in what now had been seven years of attempted price actión mastery. He also disclosed that he felt close to a solution to successful day trading. He walked briskly and stood tall that afternoon following the several hours spent reviewing his work, and his eyes had a discernible smile through the semi-thick lenses of his glasses.

### *3:45 p.m. Thursday July 26th, 1973*

The old Silver trader's swing charts proved to be an incredible aid to what had become long hours of tedious price action research and analysis. His charts revealed, in a loud and clear manner, an unmistakable swing pattern. The price swing pattern showed that higher highs were followed by higher lows and that lower lows were followed by lower highs. The pattern of higher highs, higher lows or vice versa, was broken only after a change in the trend direction of the market.

The revelation, made possible by the swing charts, was like an answer to a prayer. The implications were overwhelming, because given two swings the third swing became predictable. This principal appeared true as applied to other price data previously analyzed; so much so that three (3) choruses of hallelujah was not sufficient to express the joy of discovering the new idea. There it was, the "Lost Dutchman's Mine," the "Holy Grail," and the great "Pie In The Sky," (pursued by all commodity traders) in a single algorithm or rule that simply said that the market would attempt to repeat precisely what it had just done until repetition failed.

Hours later and well into the next morning the algorithm was checked and tested again and again. The overwhelming conclusion was that each price swing would be tradable, provided a mechanical means could be developed which would recognize the price level where one swing ended and a new swing began. In other words, the gold was there but the problem was finding the best way to get the gold mined. A problem which very nearly consumed all of the mental energy available, consistent with natural greed and educational background.

An equation resulted form the research, which provided a basis for mechanical calculation of a target for each swing which was sufficiently accurate to use for solid predictability. The equation was simple and could be solved in a few steps. The idea was a definite breakthrough and coupled with other ideas, such as common trade points, rising and falling markets, even higher-lower market openings seemed to suggest the possibilities of a single overall trading strategy; something which had eluded all deliberate previous approaches.

By 3 a.m. the excitement and thrill of imminent success at last could no longer be endured alone. Karen, precious Wife and Mother, awakened from a sound, secure sleep, listened patiently, smiled, and said, "I'm glad for you," and promptly returned to sleep. But the full significance of the equation would not be known for many months later, though the possibilities made for sweet dreams, so much so, that the market was missed entirely the next day.

### *7:05 a.m. Monday July 30th, 1973*

The Commission House regulars had shuffled into the Brokerage House consumed with trading ideas, past victories and defeats and expectations of market opportunity. They seemed dispassionate and uninterested in unsupported claims of market mastery and ultimate solution. Their lack of enthusiasm could be overlooked, however, because they were known to believe that trading commodities was nothing more than legalized gambling and not the proper subject for price action research and analysis.

The old Silver trader occupied his regular territory in the front of the room nearest the Commodity Board, his swing charts scattered and spread on his desk. He looked on patiently as he was told of the discovery and subsequent algorithm. But it was clear after a few minutes that he was anxious to begin plotting Silver prices and was not particularly interested in the why's and wherefore's of mechanical commodity trading strategies. It was with a deep sense of regret that the one trader so instrumental in the development of a new commodity trading concept, was too engrossed in his own search for a trading strategy to see what admittedly he had been searching for. As there was no other way to repay him for making his charts available, sharing the discovery of price swing predictability would have to suffice.

### *8:20 a.m. Monday August 6th, 1973*

The Burrough's programmable calculator had been attracting a lot of attention from the familiar Brokers and house regulars who had at various times crowded around or asked for individual demonstrations. The hours of constant research had led to a series of arithmetic calculations which resulted from input of three consecutive reference prices. The market was unbelievably enjoyable that morning as the calculator calculated, and the commodity prices clicked and each tended to confirm the other.

One by one they asked: What is it? How does it work? Who developed it, and does it do what it appears to do? Each in turn were told about King Neptune and his Trident which was an excellent defensive weapon against the insensitive, oft times cruel, Commodity Market. The word Trident seemed to stick somehow and became symbolic of the three pronged reality of the Commodity market, GREED, PARANOIA and EGO.

### *10:30 a.m. Christmas Day, 1973*

The Christmas tree, which had sparkled with homemade decorations, gaily wrapped gifts, and loving expectations, now resembled a paper war zone with toys, paper and miscellaneous ribbon strewn throughout the living room. The Christmas was good because the Commodity Market had given up a few of its secrets; but most of all, there were no uneasy feelings in the stomach.

***10:45 p.m. Tuesday February 5th, 1974***

The market had not gone well that morning even though Trident was applied diligently. The house was now quiet, current commodity price data lay strewn over the dining room table, and tomorrow would be a new day. Somehow, there had to be another way, a better way to avoid the pitfall of price swings which refused to stop at predictable levels. It was bitterly clear that the only thing that stood between continuous success and hit-and-miss results was additional research.

Thoughts somehow returned to former employment at an automated laboratory and a computer application to select "Peaks and Valleys," produced by auto-analyzer data recordings. The unique problem at the lab was to find the earliest moment at which the auto-analyzer voltage signal was no longer increasing, but decreasing, and vice versa over a range of zero to 4,096. The problem was not substantially different from the pattern of peaks and valleys formed by fluctuation in the market. The parallel was there, if only it could be translated in terms of real market forces. The idea struggled its way into awareness that a logical point existed when clearly a swing reversal had occurred. And that point or price represented the ideal level to enter a new trade.

Perhaps the greatest resistance to the idea came from a natural greed reaction in having to give up a portion of the new swing in favor of making certain that a new swing was established. The resistance to the new idea could have come also from a reluctance to admit an ego deflating fact; that absolute swing predictability was not possible with the technical tools thus far developed. In any event, the new idea had to be pursued.

As the time progressed into the wee hours of the morning, trial and error approaches had not led to an answer. Out of sheer desperation and frustration, empirical testing gave way to logical reasoning. On any given swing, half the traders did the right thing, the other half did the wrong thing; therefore, the only necessary thing was to be consistently part of the group that did the right thing. It was that kind of reasoning that led to the conclusion that the earliest point to enter a new trade was after a trade was 25% in progress. The idea set uneasy but represented a greed sacrifice in exchange for making money with less risk.

### *8:15 a.m. Wednesday February 6th, 1974*

The market had been very exciting so far that morning because the new entry concept tested incredibly well. Each of the several markets of interest seemed to accelerate the moment a calculated entry price was reached and rushed into immediate profit; needless to say, considerable confidence began to develop in the new entry strategy. The other traders must have been fairly curious as to why the smiles and why the exhibition of new enthusiasm for the market. But, it was premature to disclose anything to anybody.

### *2:30 p.m. Wednesday February 6th, 1974*

What had been observed that day in the market was a personal milestone, because the trades which were not taken would have yielded more than $1,700. Even though there was no trading, the tiger's tail was back in hand and there was no intention to let go. The research and testing of countless former trade entry possibilities went on in brazen competition with a noisy household and the normal demands made by small children. Karen managed to act as a buffer, but thought there would be more peace and quiet at the Library. She was absolutely right.

The Library offered unique advantages. Aside from being quiet, there were back issues of financial journals which contained an endless amount of accurate commodity price data. The Librarian mentioned that she never had a request for so many back issues of journals before, but managed to find them anyway. There was enough price data to finally give the trading strategy a rigorous test, which was something that had been lacking in the past.

***10:30 p.m. Wednesday February 6th, 1974***

The single problem which remained was: when to take optimum profit in a given trade. If there had existed an instruction to the Broker to offset the trade at the moment of maximum profit, the problem would have been resolved. But, there was no such instruction, and a strategy was needed which would have the practical effect of offsetting the trade based upon an assumption that the maximum profit had been attained.

The same logic which had rescued the research effort the previous evening could be depended upon again to solve the trade-exit problem. It became clear that the same rationale for entering a trade could apply to exiting a trade. The idea, although logical, meant an additional financial sacrifice. This thought did not sit well, because when applied to the day's $1,700 paper profit, would have reduced it to less than $1,300; a $400 sacrifice! But the logic could not be escaped and after all, it was true that making money was the object of Commodity Trading, rather than extracting each and every finite penny available in the market.

### *9:00 p.m. Friday March 29th, 1974*

Commodity Trading using the Trident strategy had become profitable and a full time job. Traveling to the Brokerage House each morning was quite a chore but it had to be considered all part of the job. An intriguing thought to establish a company with its own Commodity Price Quotation Systems consumed most of the creative moments, although no one else seemed to think that the idea had merit.

Trident was an ideal mechanical system because there was no emotional subjectivity and the arithmetic calculation could be learned by anyone: knowledge of the Commodity Market notwithstanding. Besides, a staff of Commodity Analysts could trade and monitor many more markets than one lone trader. The idea was fascinating, a new profession could be launched, and, after all, duplication of personal effort was one of the well established tenets of "How to make money."

### *6:15 a.m. Monday May 13th, 1974*

She was the second woman who had expressed interest in learning the Commodity Market. A former high school teacher with nearly grown children, her eyes were clear blue and her attitude positive even though she thought that a person had to be out of their mind to drive 35 miles half asleep, to a strange Brokerage House where no one spoke and everyone stared at a ticking Commodity Board. But she knew somehow that to learn and to master the Commodity Market could one day distinguish her as a person and as a woman.

Her task each morning as part of basic training was to select a particular commodity option and record each sequential price change. The plan was that she would become the first Commodity Analyst on what was hoped to be a good sized staff. She seemed interested but still managed to complain of the early hours and a never ending diet to lose another 25 lbs.

### *6:45 a.m. Friday September 27th, 1974*

A nervousness and uneasiness was building steadily over thoughts of the two day Trident Seminar for six brave souls who agreed to pay $250 each to learn Trident. The small staff had prepared sufficient data although they were a bit apprehensive, expressing the same ambivalent feeling that Trident should not be taught; that if the whole world knew the system, the market would be irrevocably altered, destroying once and for all the profit advantage offered by the system.

The first two students had already signed into a class which turned out to number only four. What happened to the other students will remain a mystery even though it was generally agreed later that they missed out on a very valuable experience. The Ph.D. in physics never spoke that night but looked on with an inquisitive stare. The apparently wealthy, would-be author and financial advisor type, talked incessantly about how he did things in the stock market or requested that points once covered be reviewed (A year later that same talkative student established an incredible track record of never losing a single commodity trade, even though his Broker revealed a willingness to absorb huge drops in trade equity before profit was made.) Somehow, it was 10:30 p.m. and the orientation session was over and all seemed excited and enthusiastic.

### *3:00 p.m. Monday September 30th, 1974*

The weekend class had gone well. Although small, the triumph was genuinely shared by the students as well as the staff. The decision to continue teaching the system was made. The office had proved adequate, although there had been complaints over the small 24" by 30" blackboard. The staff expressed mild concern that the larger classes hoped for would require larger facilities.

Perhaps, the most remarkable thing about that first class was the fact that the only student who had traded commodities before was the physicist, who seemed quite pleased and delighted that he finally had a trading strategy that made "good sense." The key premise of Trident was that knowledge of the commodity market was not a prerequisite for learning the system. The other three students had always wanted to trade commodities but could never find anyone willing to teach them how. The future seemed bright indeed.

### *1:45 p.m. Thursday November 21st, 1974*

They said that anyone bold enough to call on a daily basis could participate in the Chart Talk section of the Teletyped Commodity News. By that time Trident had been taught during several classes and appeared to be an ideal trading system for calling specific trades that could be executed during the next day's trading session.

The challenge to prove the constant power of Trident to a skeptical Commodity world was unbearably exquisite, even though the alternate possibility for failure hid in those certain recesses of mind and stomach. With positive attitude and a certain degree of pressure, a format was developed, which would clearly define all specific trades and at the same time communicate a somewhat foreign Trident language.

### *1:05 p.m. Monday December 9th, 1974*

The expected call for input to the next day's Chart Talk had arrived and it was time to put it together with specific trades in Silver, Cocoa and Wheat.

| | | | | | | |
|---|---|---|---|---|---|---|
| SELL | — | Feb Silver | 4.245 | Stop. | Target | 4.162 |
| BUY | — | Mar Cocoa | 64.80 | Stop. | Target | 68.90 |
| SELL | — | Mar Wheat | 4.84 1/2 | Stop. | Target | 4.78-3/4 |

It was discovered several weeks later that in spite of the 17 trades offered between December 9th, 1974 and January 2nd, 1975, very few Commodity Traders across the country knew or cared one way or another, other than a perceptive few, who managed to call and inquire whether or not Advisory Services were available. Each caller was told the same; no Advisory Service available.

Even though there had been an obvious lack of interest in Chart Talk, Trident did manage to establish its first track record which could not be refuted.

| Total Trades | Total Wins | Win Amt. | % Win | Total Losses | Loss Amt. | % Loss | Net Profit | Net Effective |
|---|---|---|---|---|---|---|---|---|
| 17 | 14 | $8,740. | 82% | 3 | $708. | 18% | $8,032. | 92% |

# PRICE ACTION THEORY

# CHAPTER 2

## BACKGROUND

The commodity market is influenced by many forces, real and imagined. Railroad strikes and rumors of strikes, political coups and rumors of coups, hog cholera, droughts, crop damage and floods, facts and fiction, all play a role in the millions of individual decisions to buy or sell commodities. All events, real or imagined, are thought to impact on either future supply or future demand, and accordingly cause market price fluctuation as traders and speculators react to these events and rumors.

If all commodity traders heard the facts and rumors and interpreted them the same way, they would all buy or sell together. Usually, however, traders hear different facts and rumors, and interpret these facts and rumors differently. The fact that there are always buyers and sellers for the same market attests to these differences. At the time a rumor is circulated, it is impossible to assess how correct the rumor is and if it is correct, the extent to which it will influence current market prices.

The commodity market exists for one and only one reason, and that reason is to ***make money.*** Making money is the single common idea that joins all the various market forces together. A very important force in the market is ***GREED***. Since people trade commodities to make money, it is understandable that they want to make as much money as possible.

Greed can be a trader's worst enemy because it causes traders to remain in trades too long, or might cause a trader to terminate a trade too soon. Sometimes GREED causes a trader to become irrational, paranoiac and illogical. This can and does result in loss of profits, or loss of capital. For reasons best left to psychologists, it is difficult to control greed.

The Trident Trading System was developed to remedy the problems of rumor and greed. The system acknowledges the fact that rumors are plentiful forces in the market, and that no one is ever in full knowledge of the correctness of these rumors. In order to escape the devastating effects of believing the "wrong rumor," the system ignores rumors. The only events which the system acknowledges are the trader's net reaction to rumors and news events (Price events). These reactions are reflected by the daily price fluctuations in the market. Trident is concerned solely with price fluctuation. As such, Trident is an objective trading strategy which determines future prices only on the basis of past and current prices.

The commodity market consists of essentially four distinct trader groups. It is the buying and selling activities of these trader groups which establish price events upon which the Trident Trading Strategy depends. The following four trader groups make up the commodity market:

**PRODUCERS:** The owner or producer of commodities participates in trade transactions in order to minimize the risk of commodity price deterioration prior to market time. Those who actually produce the commodity (farmer, rancher, miner, etc.) make money through protecting attractive profit margins between the current futures price and the cost of production. Producers most often operate as large seller (short hedge) as a safeguard against the risks of price decline.

**COMMERCIAL PROCESSOR:** The processor of commodities participates in trade transactions in order to reduce the risk of higher prices eroding his profit margin should the supply situation change substantially beyond his forecast. Processors reduce the risk essentially in an opposite way than that of the Producer, namely, by buying (long hedge) the futures contract. Only through trading commodities can the Processor provide a safeguard against lack of adequate future supply.

**FLOOR TRADERS:** The floor trader is essentially a speculator either for his own account or for the account of someone else. Trading floors of various Commodity Exchanges are the hectic, oft times chaotic outcry auction scene through which futures contracts are traded. There are three categories of floor traders; floor brokers who fill orders for commission houses (Brokerage firms) and commercial interests receiving a fee for each transaction. Speculators, who buy and sell for their own account, either as Day Traders or as Position Traders; and scalpers, who trade for short-term profits during the course of each trading session.

**COMMISSION HOUSE SPECULATORS:** The Commission House speculator trades commodities through brokerage firms expressly for the opportunity to make money. Their opportunity is created through the daily actions of those who must participate in the commodity market in order to minimize the risk of handling commodities. Commission house speculators are active buyers or sellers depending upon their judgement as to which is the best opportunity to realize a profit. (Unfortunately, the vast majority of these speculators lose rather than make money, very much the same way people lose at the race track or gambling in Las Vegas.)

It is the combined interaction of these trader-groups which causes commodity price fluctuation. Buying, selling, hedging and spreading are all done in the name of making money, to the extent that commodity markets account for the greatest money-volume enterprise in the world. Each trader-group, trading for reasons known and unknown, creates price action, i.e., wide price swings, narrow trade ranges, reversals, consolidation, gaps, active trading sessions and inactive trading sessions. And, in many instances, create their own self-fulfilling prophecy by believing that the market is doing one thing, when in fact, it is doing the complete opposite.

## PRICE FLUCTUATION, TRENDS, SWINGS

There is a fundamental idea common to the Commodity, Stock, Bond, Option, Currency, and other actively traded markets. That idea is that prices fluctuate (change). Prices fluctuate upward. Prices fluctuate downward. Prices fluctuate sideways. Prices fluctuate at different levels at the same time.

Price fluctuation (Figure 1) is associated with a trend direction. A trend direction can be described as Up or Down, and sometimes sideways (flat). Once a trend direction is established, price fluctuation will continue in that direction until the highest or lowest price in that direction is reached.

(The idea of price fluctuation in a trend direction is not new. This idea was known and noted by the earliest price action theorists (Tubbs). Chartists depend upon charts and graphs in order to

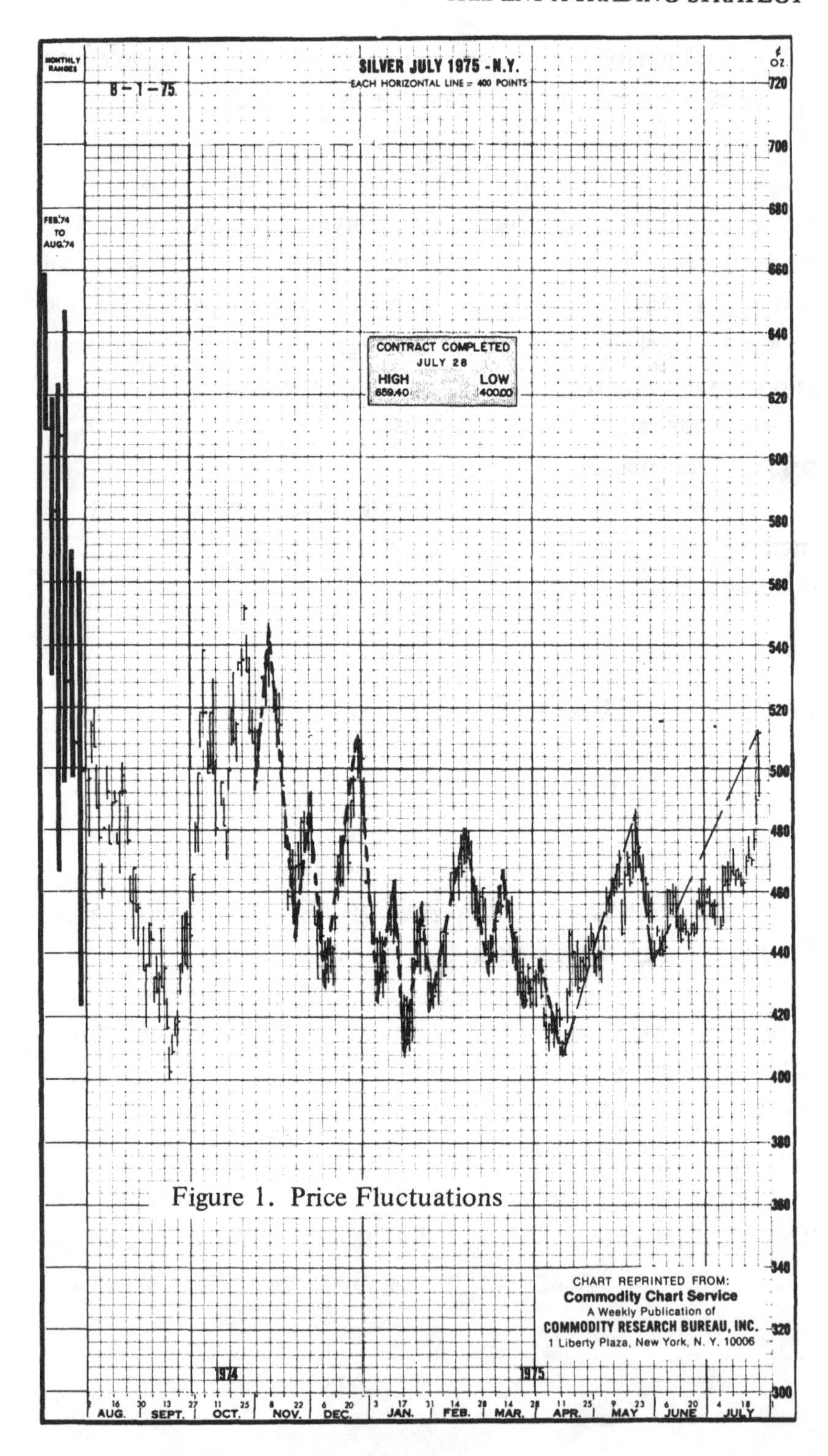


Figure 1. Price Fluctuations

monitor price trend progress and changes. Most technical tools, including computerized systems, depend upon price fluctuation and trend analysis.)

> **DEFINITION:** Price fluctuation in the same trend direction is equivalent to a single continuous price change called a price swing, joining the lowest price in the trend to the highest price in the trend or vice versa depending upon trend direction. (Figure 1 reveals a series of price swings which illustrate the concept of price continuity.)

## MARKET PRESSURE

Price action in the market reflects the ongoing struggle between Buy-Sell transactions. The price of a commodity futures contract fluctuates up and down steadily according to buying or selling pressure exerted by the traders. Whenever buying pressure exceeds selling pressure, the price fluctuates upward. Whenever selling pressure exceeds buying pressure, the price fluctuates downward. If buying pressure equals selling pressure, the price will remain constant.

The Trident Trading Strategy is based upon unique prices at which buying pressure is overcome by selling pressure and selling pressure is overcome by buying pressure. These prices are significant because they represent the net reactions of all traders as reflected through the sentiment to buy or sell and which idea is the most predominant. A ***Trident Price*** is therefore the price at which buying or selling pressure is overcome by the other. (See Figures 2, 3 & 4.)

Consider (see Figure 5), $P_1$ representing the price at which buying pressure overcomes selling pressure. Then $P_2$ would represent the price at which selling pressure overcame buying pressure. The price move between $P_1$ and $P_2$ is called ***A SWING***. Swings occur constantly and can be expressed as a law of the market.

## PRICE SWINGS

Commodity prices can be considered as unstable as surf and wave action at the beach. Commodity price instability is called fluctuation (change). At first glance, price fluctuation appears to be random and some researchers have concluded that due to the apparent random nature of price fluctuation, commodity prices cannot be predicted, or more simply, "There's no way to predict future prices."

Trident, as a basis for analysis of commodity price action, is designed to permit the seemingly random price fluctuation to lend itself to positive logical predictability. Through specific analysis of price action, predictability models can be constructed which are not random in any particular way.

> **DEFINITION:** When buying overtakes selling, causing the commodity price to fluctuate upward, then such upward trend will continue until selling overcomes buying with the result being a price swing from some "low" to some "high." (The opposite is also true.)

A price swing can therefore be considered a continuous move either up or down (rising or falling), establishing highs and lows in alternate sequence.

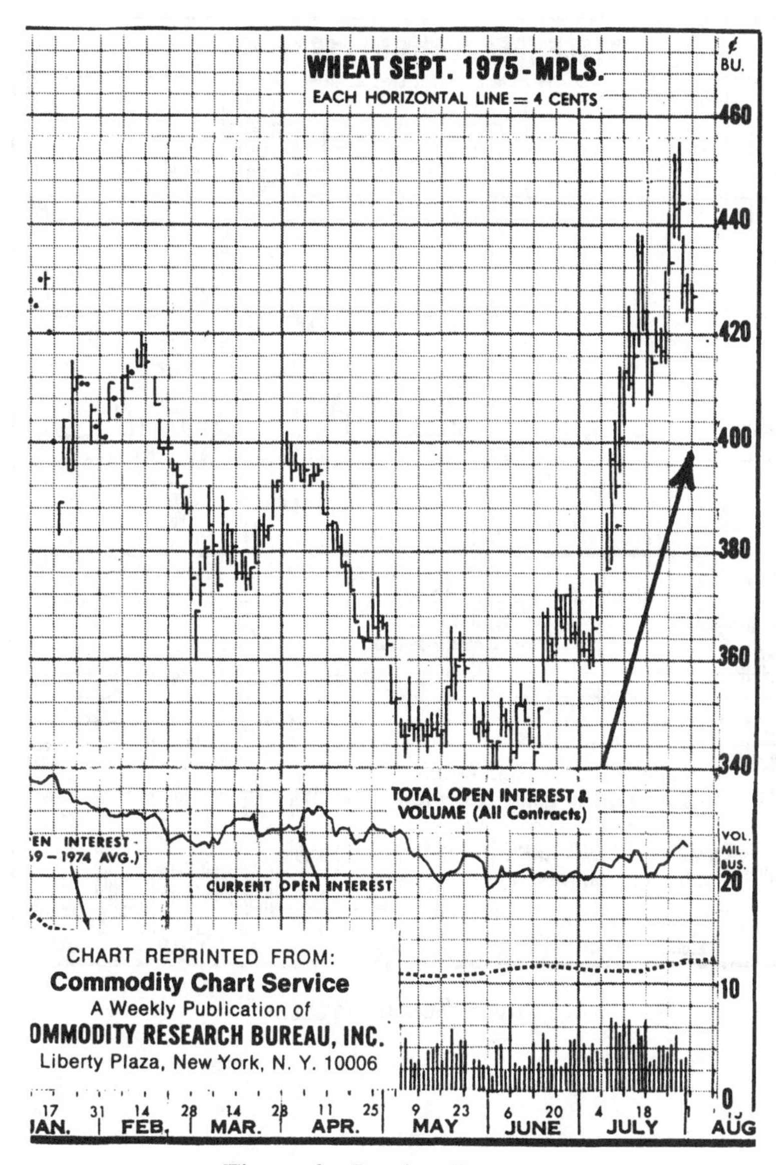


Figure 2. Buying Pressure

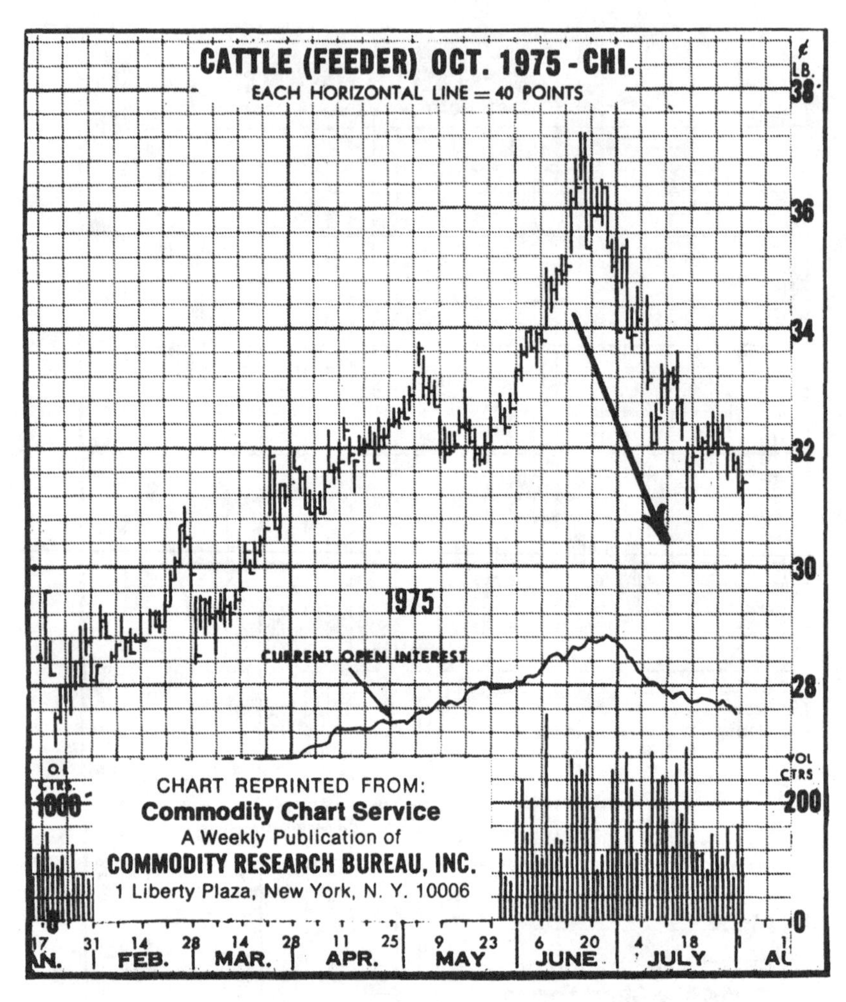


Figure 3. Selling Pressure

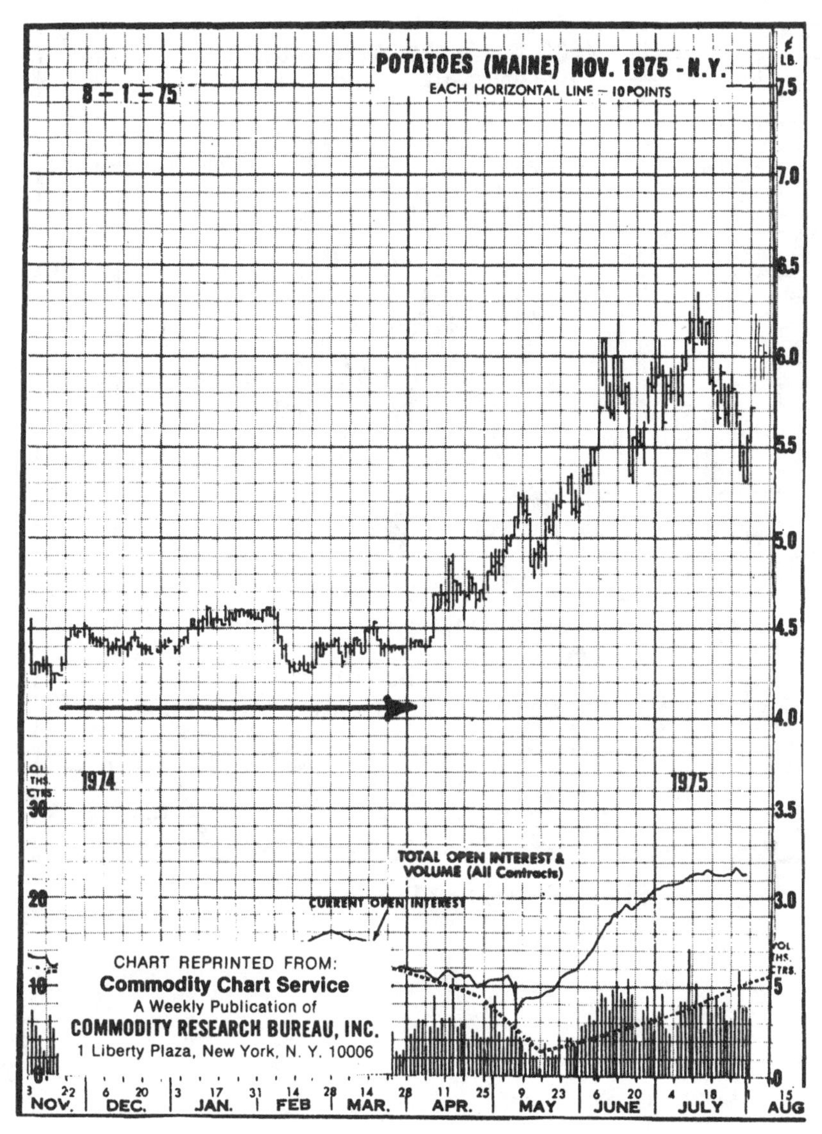


Figure 4. Buying Pressure Equal Selling Pressure

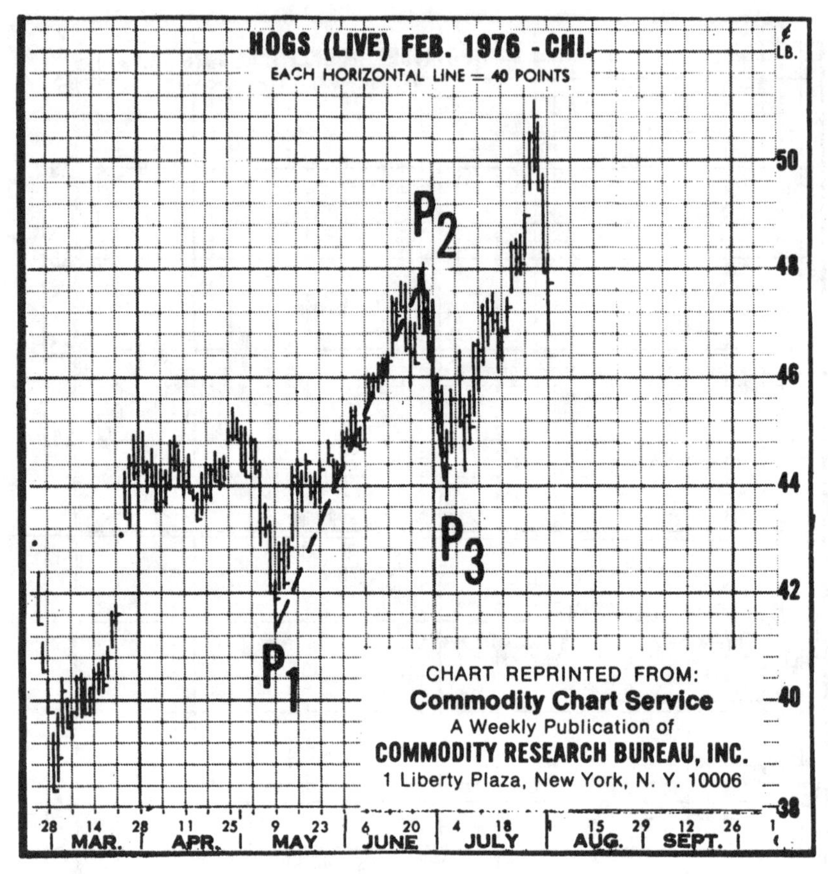


Figure 5. Trident Prices (Buying)

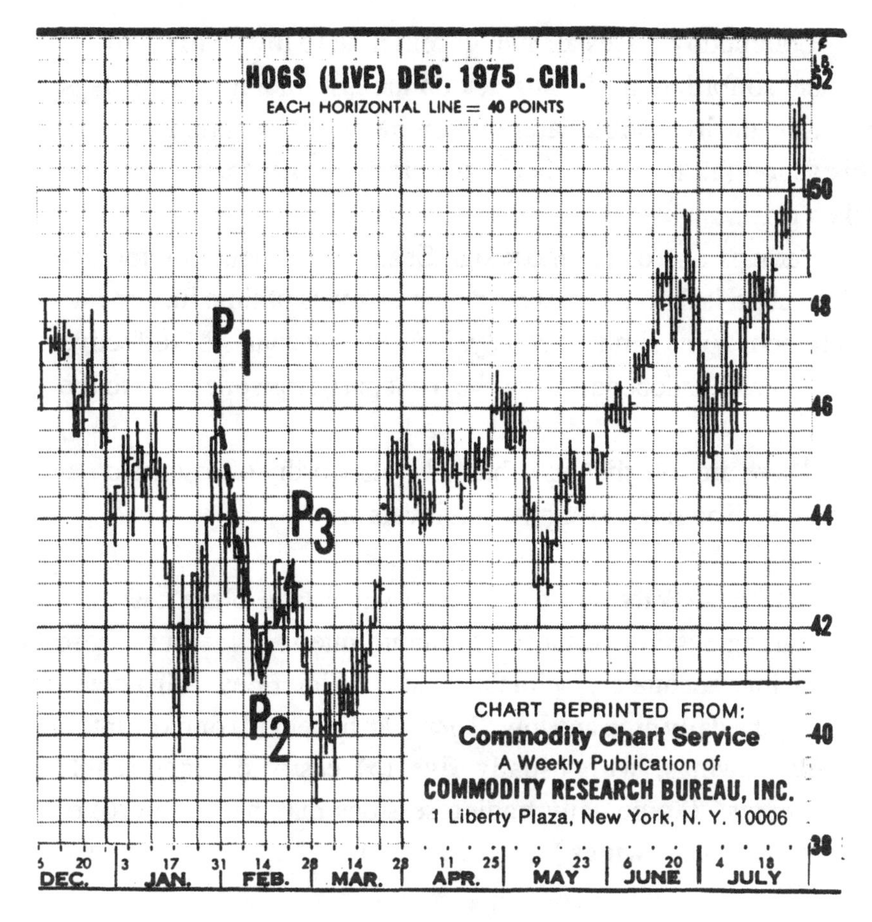


Figure 6. Trident Prices (Selling)

Commodity prices all swing from high to low to high to low . . . and so forth until the last tick on the last trading day. This is precisely the irresistible nature of commodity price action. Should this action fail to occur, then it is axiomatic that trading has not taken place.

Perhaps one of the most significant facts about commodity price action is that it occurs over several levels of time increments continuously and simultaneously. Yet, Trident analysis is effective at each level, independent, for the most part, from one level to the next.

There are five distinguishable levels worthy of discussion at this time. The five (5) significant levels are:

**MICROSWINGS:** Inter-day swings take place during a trading session (usually 15 minute intervals measure these swings adequately) with the maximum inter-day swing creating the daily high and low. There can be four (4) or more inter-day swings, with usually five (5) easily distinguishable swings. (Some daily trading sessions may have ten (10) or more micro-swings.) (See Table 1.)

**MINOR SWINGS:** Sequential daily highs and lows produce continuous swings from some daily high or low to some other daily high or low. The key to minor swings is to measure from the highest daily high to the lowest daily low in sequence. Then repeat this from the lowest daily low to the highest daily high in sequence. Minor swings can be expected to occur over periods ranging from one to five or more days. (See Figure 7.)

**INTERMEDIATE SWINGS:** Sequential minor swings (highs, lows) produce continuous intermediate swings ranging

**WHEAT – SEPTEMBER 1975**

| | | | | | | | | | | | |
|---|---|---|---|---|---|---|---|---|---|---|---|
| 3.66 | 3.65½ | (3.65) | 3.65½ | (3.66) | 3.65 | 3.64½ | (3.63½) | 3.64 | 3.65 | 3.64½ | 3.65 |
| 3.65½ | 3.64½ | 3.65 | 3.66 | 3.66½ | 3.66 | 3.66½ | 3.67 | 3.68 | 3.68½ | 3.68 | (3.68½) |
| 3.68 | 3.67 | 3.66 | (3.65) | 3.66 | 3.67½ | 3.68 | 3.69½ | 3.70 | 3.69½ | 3.70 | 3.71 |
| (3.73) | 3.72½ | 3.70 | 3.69 | (3.68½) | 3.70 | 3.69 | 3.69½ | (3.70) | 3.69½ | 3.69 | 3.68½ |
| 3.68 | 3.67 | (3.66) | 3.68 | 3.69 | 3.68½ | 3.68 | 3.68½ | 3.69 | 3.68½ | 3.69 | 3.70 |
| 3.71 | 3.71½ | 3.72 | 3.73 | 3.72 | 3.72½ | 3.73 | (3.74)* | 3.73 | 3.72½ | 3.73 | 3.72½ |
| 3.73½ | 3.73 | 3.72 | (3.71½) | 3.72 | 3.73 | (3.73½) | 3.72 | 3.71½ | 3.71 | (3.70) | 3.70½ |
| 3.71 | 3.70 | 3.71 | 3.72 | 3.71½ | 3.72 | 3.72¼ | 3.72½ | 3.73 | 3.72½ | (3.73) | 3.72 |
| 3.72½ | 3.72 | 3.72½ | 3.72 | 3.71½ | 3.71 | 3.72 | 3.71 | 3.70 | 3.69 | 3.70 | 3.70½ |
| 3.70 | 3.69 | 3.68½ | 3.68 | 3.66 | (3.65) | 3.66 | 3.65 | 3.65½ | 3.66 | 3.67 | (3.67½ |
| 3.66 | 3.65½ | 3.65 | (3.63) | (3.65) | 3.64 | 3.63½ | 3.63 | 3.62½ | 3.62* | | |

( * indicates high-low of the day)

Table 1. Micro Swings

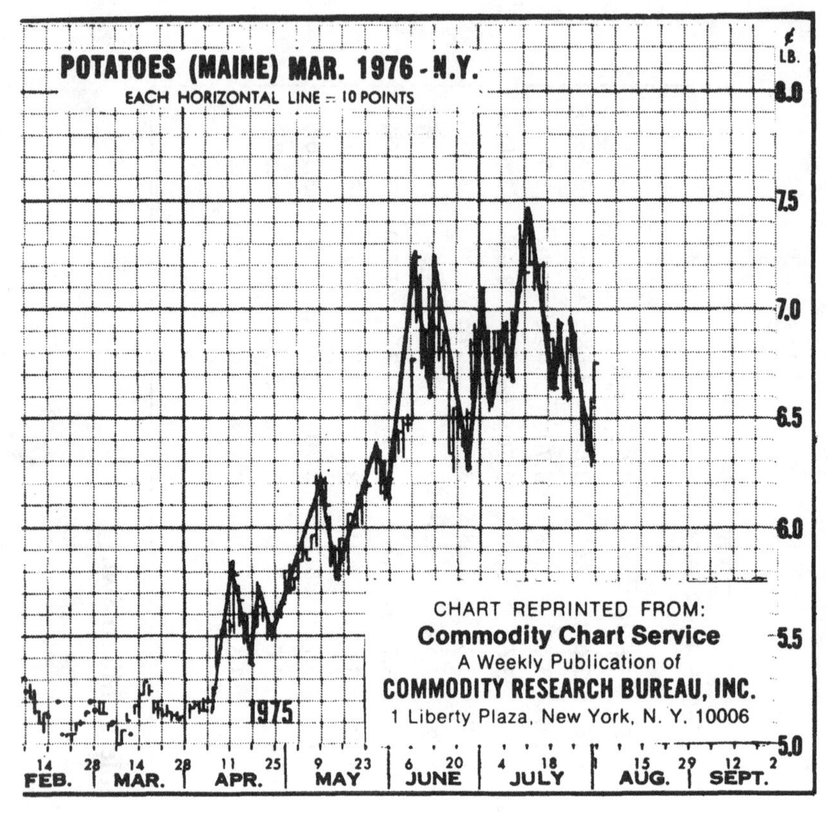


Figure 7. Minor Swings

from the highest minor high to the lowest minor low in sequence and from the lowest minor low to the highest minor high in sequence. Intermediate swings generally form over a period of a week or two. Intermediate swings signal the trend change of minor swings and represent a good level for successful commodity trading. (See Figure 8.)

**MAJOR SWINGS:** Sequential intermediate swings (highs, lows) produce continuous major swings ranging from the highest intermediate high to the lowest intermediate low in sequence and from the lowest intermediate low to the highest intermediate high in sequence. Major swings set the trend direction of a particular commodity market (all contracts). Major swings represent another good investment opportunity as they generally require months to form. (See Figure 9.)

**MASTER SWINGS:** Sequential life of contract highs and lows form the basis for master swings. These swings require years to form. For this reason they do not represent Trident trading opportunities because entry and exit of trades would involve different contract options. Individuals who look to the commodity market as an investment vehicle should be aware, however, of the master swing status relative to their long term position.

The relationship between Micro-Major swings is such that a major high or low is always an intermediate high or low; and is always a minor high or low; and is always a micro high or low; and is al-ways a single tick change in commodity price fluctuation.

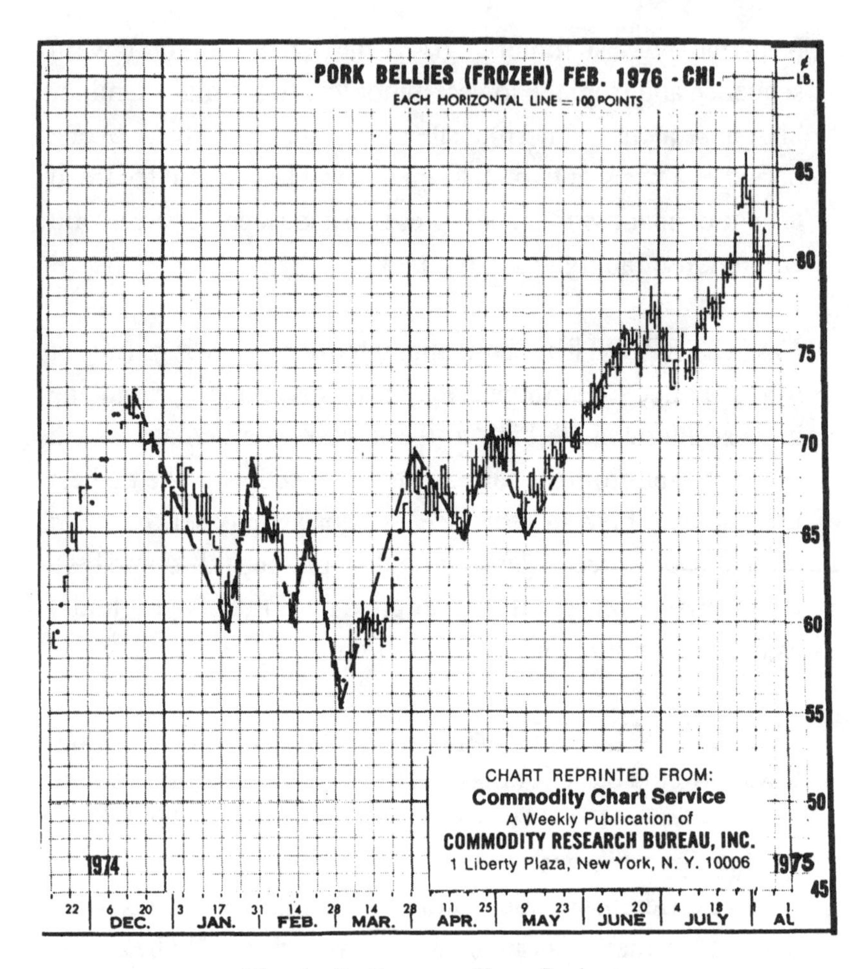


Figure 8. Intermediate Swings

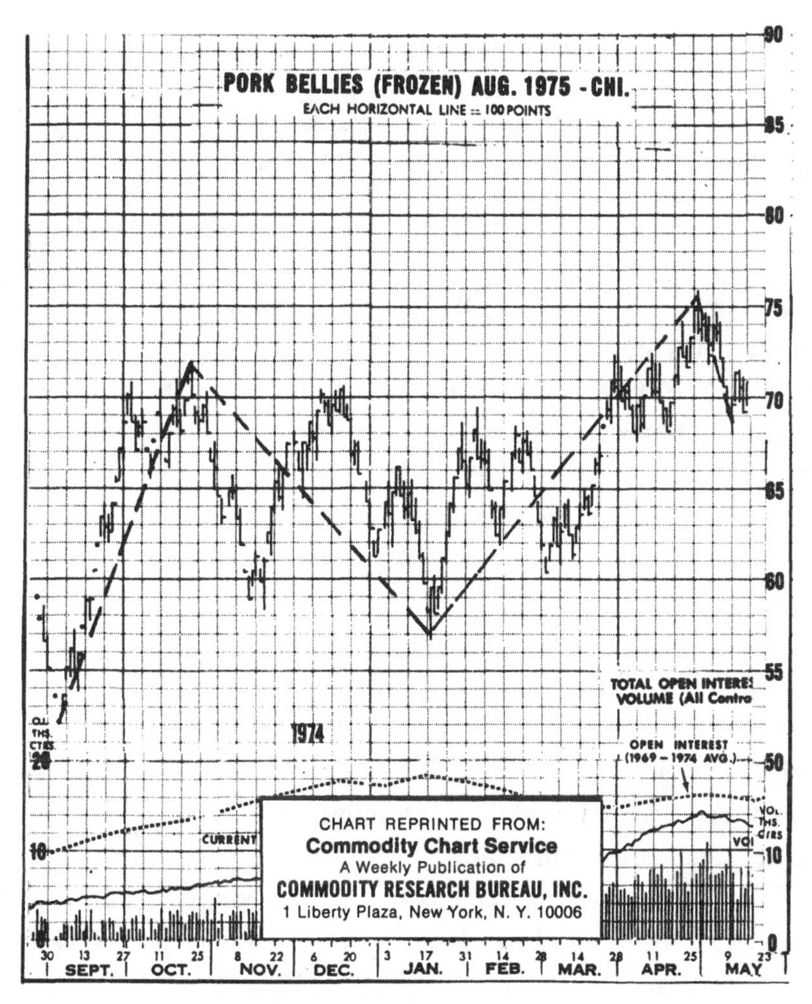


Figure 9. Major Swings

## BASIC CONCEPTS

Trident is a trading strategy which incorporates a series of assumptions, rules and arithmetic formulas designed to remove guesswork and risk from the market. It is intended to reduce trading to a disciplined mechanical (non-emotional) financial pursuit. A certain degree of objectivity is needed in order to overcome ego, especially in the area of concern over being right or wrong (only the market is right). Trident permits the trader to make money even though the trade was wrong. In that sense, Trident fulfills the purpose for trading, which is making money.

The Trident Trading Strategy is based upon the assumption that:

***"THE FUTURE IS BASED UPON THE IMMEDIATE PAST"***

An idea not particularly new, but when applied to price action in the market becomes the basis for predicting (Forecasting) what the market can be expected to do.

The future price of a commodity can be thought of as the net effect of past causes such as: Buy or Sell transactions, profit taking, stop loss protection, contingent orders, rumors, reports, news events, inaction, and a multiple of other considerations. Accordingly, current price (last price quoted) is the right price consistent with the combined reactions of all ***active*** traders. Future price, therefore, can be thought of as an immediate consequence of current price and is nothing more than the sequential update (balancing) of current price. Therefore, ***FUTURE PRICE IS THE EFFECT CAUSED BY CURRENT PRICE.***

The "immediate past" also contains trader reactions, decisions and ideas, which will be acted upon in future time (compensation). Since all traders are not available for market transactions at the same time, the current price merely represents the balance of those available at a particular time. Consider, therefore, that the current price reflects only a percentage of all potential trader action. The balance of total trader reaction must be viewed as a combination of ***current price*** plus ***future price*** in order to create a basic model of price action consistent with ***how*** and ***why*** price fluctuates.

Price predictability is the ultimate goal of all commodity traders. The Trident Trading Strategy contains an assumptive prediction base predicated on price swing continuity. The basic assumption is that price swings are tradeable. Therefore, given the existence of price swings and the fact that price swings are tradeable, a fundamental strategy emerges. The only conditions for tradability involve swing recognition and trade selection.

# THE TRIDENT MODEL

# CHAPTER 3

Commodity trading is a serious business. Large sums of money are won and lost every trading day. The greatest advantage a commodity trader can have is a serious business-like personal attitude towards the market. Too many commodity traders approach the market as though commodity trading were a game of chance. Such an attitude has no relevance to the serious business of making money.

Applying a rigorous mechanical discipline to the commodity market, successfully, requires deliberate non-emotional thinking. Each concept, rule and equation described in this chapter is designed to create a low risk reliable trading strategy. The entire basis for Trident is to create more profitable trades than losing trades. The idea that a commodity trader should expect many small losses and a few compensating large gains perpetuates the game of chance point-of-view. Obviously, a better idea is many profitable trades with few losing trades. For this reason, the Trident Trading Strategy has built in odds, 3 to 1 in favor of the trader.

## THE MODEL

The Trident model consists of a collection of arithmetic formulas deduced from analysis of price swings and price action. The key idea expressed in the model is:

***"ONE AND ONLY ONE IDEAL TRADE EXISTS FOR EACH PRICE SWING WHOSE OBJECTIVE IS AN IDEAL TARGET FOR THAT PRICE SWING."***

Emphasis is placed on the concept of "IDEAL" because Trident analysis does not represent an exact science but rather a set of unique assumptions which provide for contingent action.

The price swing P3 to P4 (Figure 10), depicts one and only one best trade: buy at P3 and sell at P4. The price swing P3 to P4 (Figure 11) likewise, indicates one and only one best trade: sell at P3, buy at P4. If traders knew the precise price level at which buy-sell pressure would reverse itself, then trading would be risk-free and probably outlawed forever.

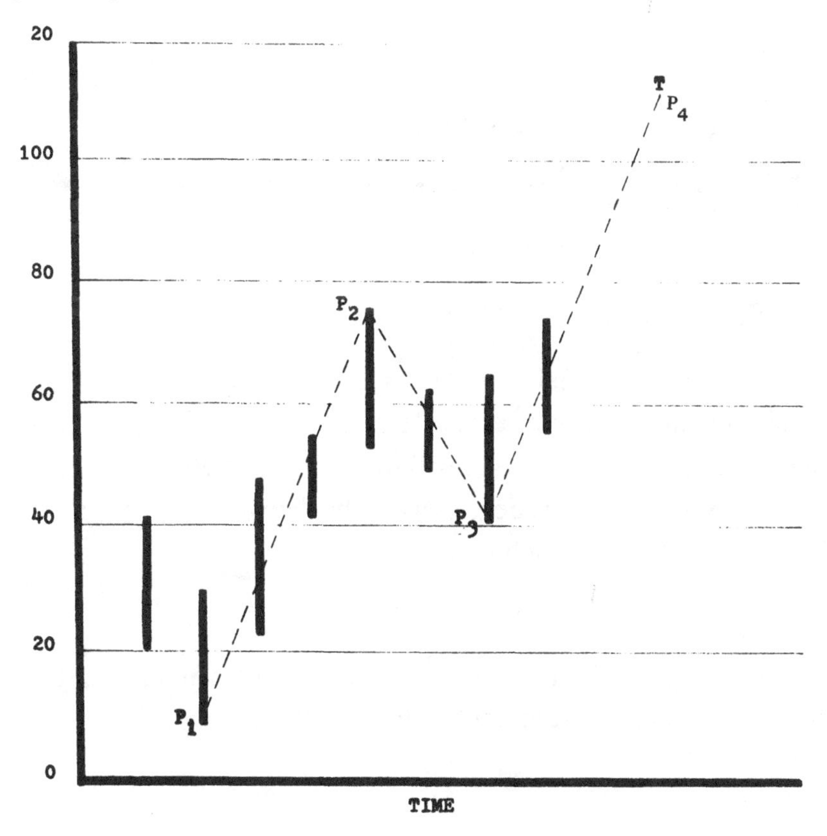


Figure 10. Ideal Targets (Rising)

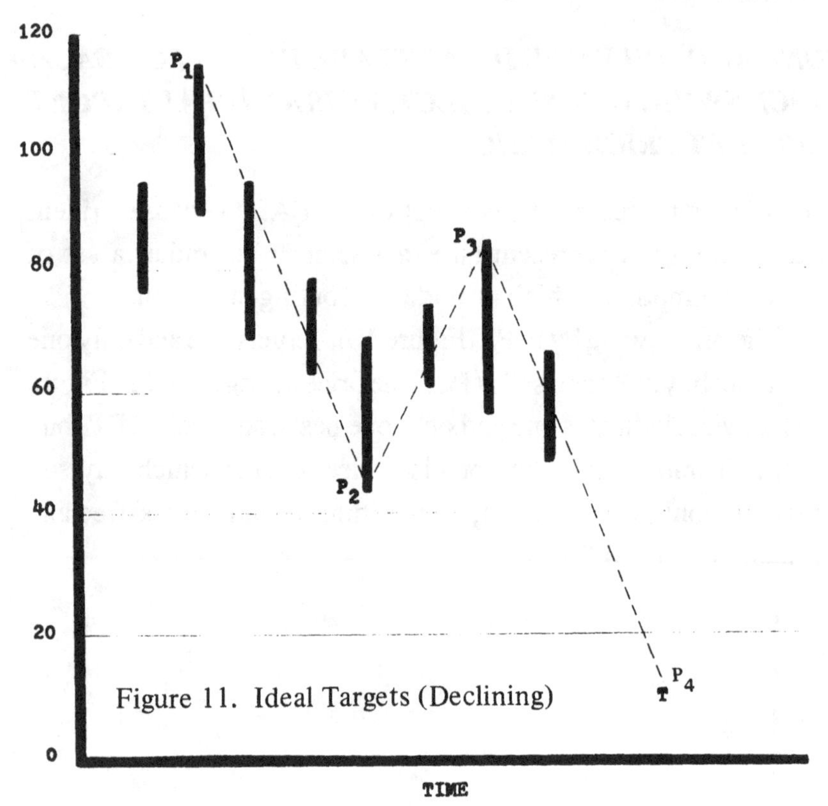


Figure 11. Ideal Targets (Declining)

## TRIDENT SWING TARGETS

The Trident model operates as a simulator based upon the assumption that: "the future is based upon the immediate past," and therefore, the next price swing will resemble the previous swing in the same direction. Consider a relationship between $P_1$, $P_2$, $P_3$ and $P_4$ (Figures 10 & 11) such that:

$$P_1 + P_4 = P_2 + P_3$$

If $P_1$, $P_2$ and $P_3$ represents known actual swing prices, then $P_4$ represents the ideal target for the next (future) swing. Then it follows that:

$$P_4 = P_2 + P_3 - P_1$$

Let $P_4$ = Target T then:

$$T = P_2 + P_3 - P_1$$

The target (T) operates as an ideal target, that is, a price level forecast rather than a hard fact or absolute prediction. It is not necessary for Trident targets to be reached and, in many instances, the targets are not reached.

Trident targets exist for every swing at each swing level. The Trident algorithm holds true for calculating Major swing targets as well as Micro swing targets. The important fact is that one algorithm works for all levels. A fact which suggests that price action is not random, but on the contrary quite deliberate and symmetric. (Price action symmetry has been the subject of researchers for the last four decades with only partial positive results.)

The market contains numerous examples of Trident formation and target completion. Consider the example (Figure 12):

$$\begin{aligned}
P_1 &= 63.50,\ P_2 = 76.40,\ P_3 = 71.40 \\
T &= P_2 + P_3 - P_1 \\
&= 76.40 + 71.40 - 63.50 \\
&= 147.80 - 63.50 \\
\boxed{T} &\boxed{= 84.30}
\end{aligned}$$

In this example, the swing from P3 to T occurred exactly as predicted, i.e., the intermediate price swing terminated at 84.30. (The move from P3 to T was 1290 points or $4,744.00 a sum worthy of the few minutes of analysis required by the trading strategy). However, Trident targets merely represent directional

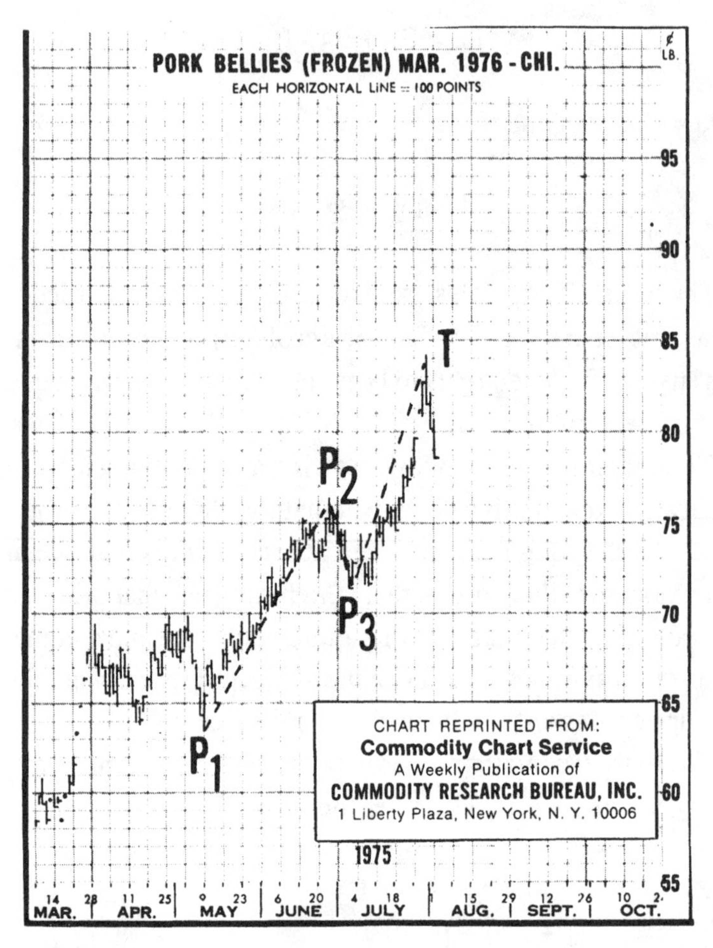


Figure 12. Perfect Intermediate Target Development

ideas rather than absolute predictions. In practice, targets are reached or exceeded approximately 40% of the time (statistic is based upon several hundred samples).

Market trend direction is not a factor for Trident targets (Figure 13). Consider this example of a down target:

$$P_1 = 4.04, P_2 = 3.36, P_3 = 3.88$$

$$T = P_2 + P_3 - P_1$$

$$= 3.36 + 3.88 - 3.36$$

$$= 7.24 - 4.04$$

$$\boxed{T = 3.20}$$

## ACTION vs REACTION

The trading floor of Commodity Exchanges can best be described as "organized chaos." Floor traders through open outcry and hand signals buy and sell commodities in absolute glorious competition, each attempting to get the best price execution. Some trading pits are fairly inactive while other pits swarm with traders furiously involved in hot competition. Floor traders know from years of experience to "go where the action is," and that's exactly what happens.

The Trident model recognizes action also, but only in a technical sense. The action in any market is where the best opportunity for profit exists. Since the future reflects the past, it follows that direct observation of "the immediate past" will indicate which side of the market yields the most profit.

The reaction to a profitable trade should be to take a profit. A Hedger reacts to a price level by locking in profit. Some speculators and Scalpers react by "counter-punching" the move. In general,

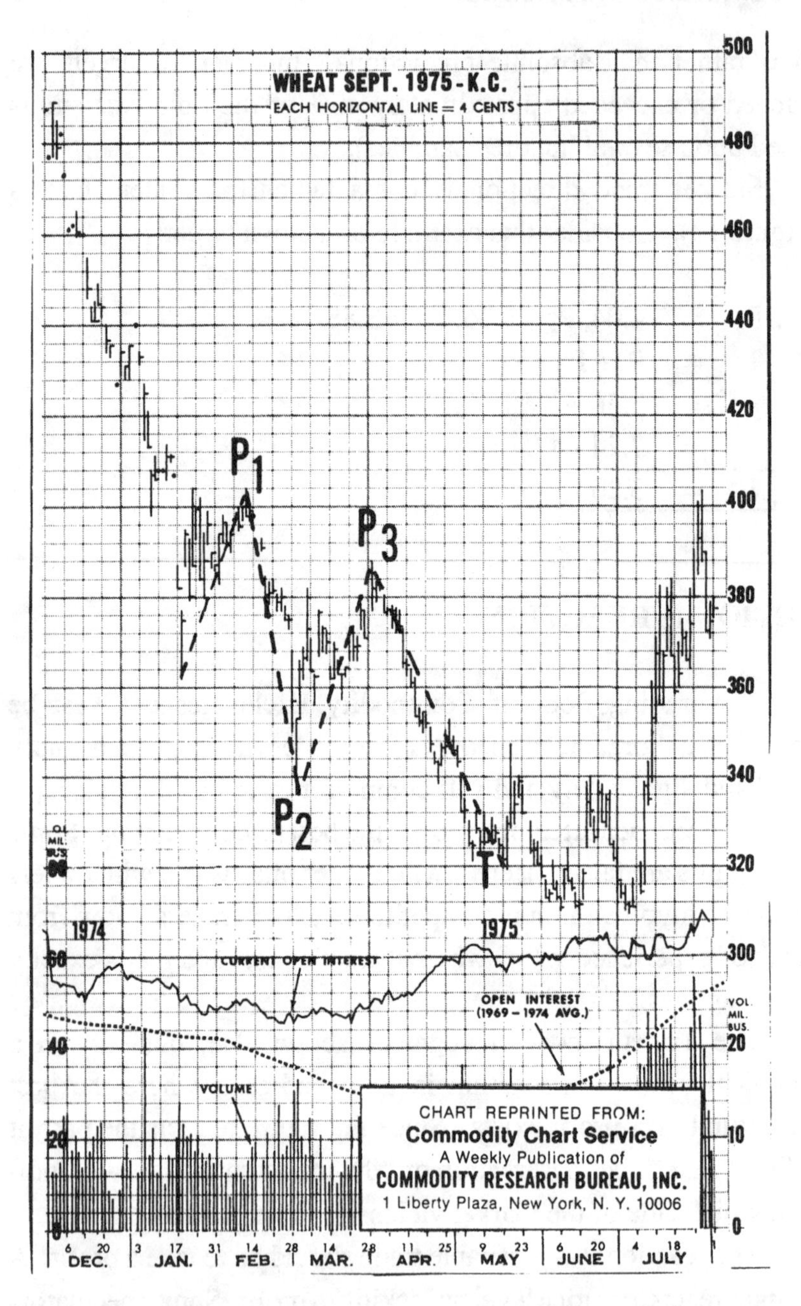


Figure 13. Trident Target Development

however, profit-taking is a reaction rather than an initial action. The Trident Trading rules are:

***"IN AN UP-MARKET, PRICE SWINGS TO THE UPSIDE YIELD GREATER PROFITS THAN THE SWINGS TO THE DOWNSIDE."***

***"IN A DOWN-MARKET, PRICE SWINGS TO THE DOWNSIDE YIELD GREATER PROFITS THAN THE SWINGS TO THE UPSIDE."***

However, the basic rule to remember is:

***"TRADE THE ACTION, NOT THE REACTION."***

Reaction swings (Figures 14 & 15) should not be traded because the risk-reward ratio of such trades amounts to an "out and out gamble," ***something to be definitely avoided.*** Market reactions (dips or rallies) are generally short lived and abrupt. Accordingly, only action swings present good trading opportunity, and, therefore, ***only half the swings within a given trade level should be traded.***

## ENTRY

Determining the initial ***BUY*** or ***SELL*** price is a matter of knowing when a new price swing has started. As one swing completes itself, the next swing starts. And so forth, at each swing level, until the last price tick. But the problem remains; how to determine the start of the next price swing?

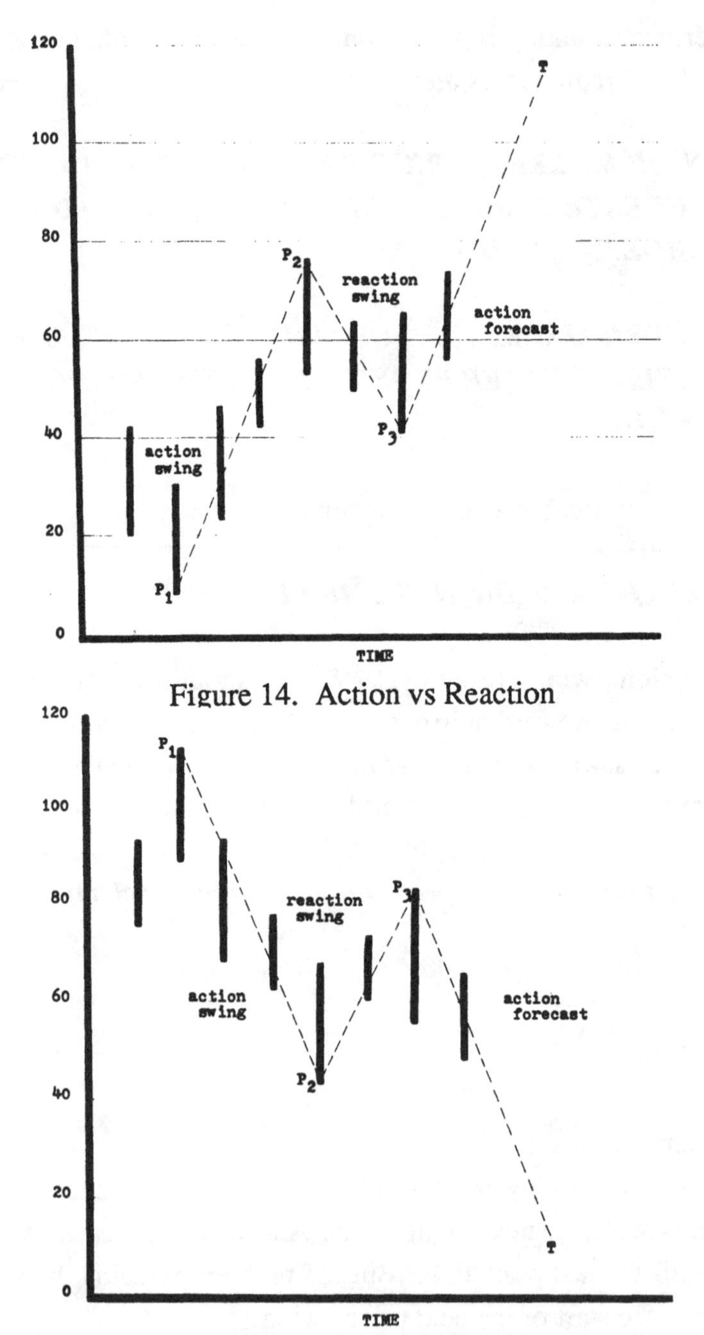


Figure 14. Action vs Reaction



Figure 15. Action vs Reaction

The problem of recognizing new price swings early enough to take advantage of them is the same problem of picking peaks and valleys; i.e., when can $P_2$ be defined as a peak, and when can $P_3$ be defined as a valley (Figure 16)?

The skill developed in understanding that swings are constantly occurring and therefore must be anticipated will prove to be very profitable for the average Trident trader.

During the price swing $P_1$ to $P_2$ (Figure 16), the "ONE AND ONLY ONE" best trade was to buy at P1 and later sell at $P_2$. Those traders who bought at $P_1$ were the correct traders, while those who bought at $P_2$ were incorrect. The average of those correct buyers and those incorrect buyers is at a price midway between $P_1$ and $P_2$. The mid-point $(P_1 + P_2)/2$ divides correct buying action from incorrect buying action. Consider only those traders in the correct buying group, that is, those who bought between $P_1$ and $(P_1 + P_2)/2$; then the average correct buyer bought mid-way between $P_1$ and $(P_1 + P_2)/2$, or, at the price $P_1 + (P_1 + P_2)/4$. The converse would be true also for correct selling (Figure 17).

During the next action swing $P_3$ to $P_4$ (Figure 16), the average correct price level to buy would be the same distance from $P_3$ as it was from $P_1$ during the previous action swing. And this is precisely the Trident entry price concept:

$$\text{ENTRY PRICE} = \frac{(P_2 - P_1)}{4} + P_3 \qquad (2)$$

But then, this price is simply a price 25% away from $P_3$ on the way to $P_4$ (Target). It is this 25% price level that represents the earliest time to determine that the previous price swing has terminated in either a peak or a valley; and a new price swing has started. (Note that equation (2) "entry price" will hold true for either buying or selling transactions.)

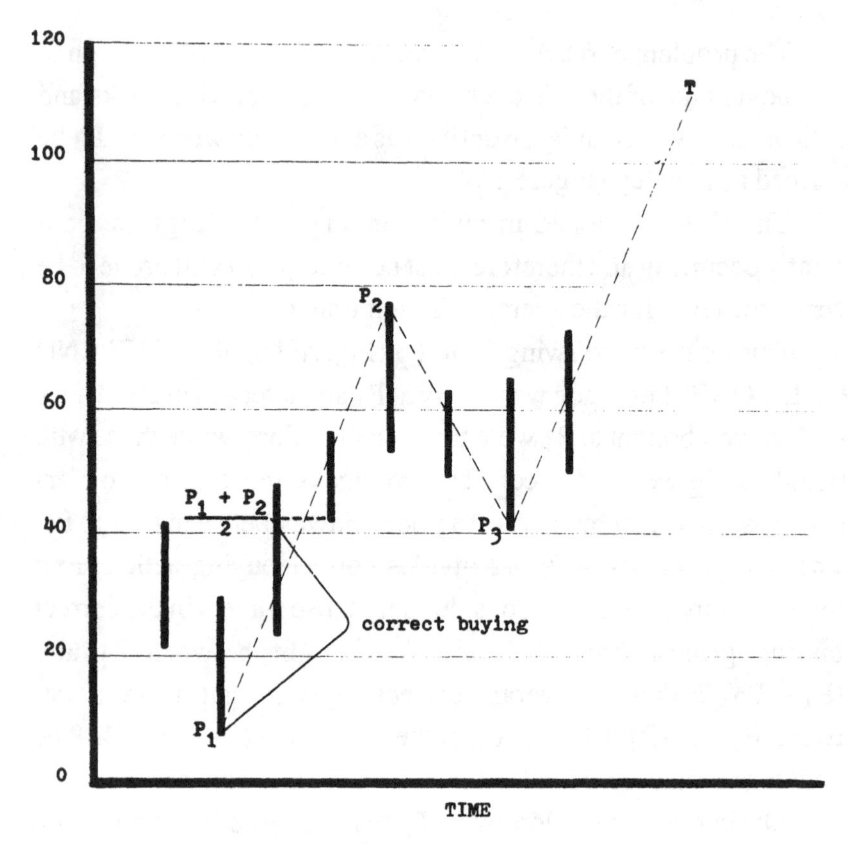


Figure 16. Correct Buying Region

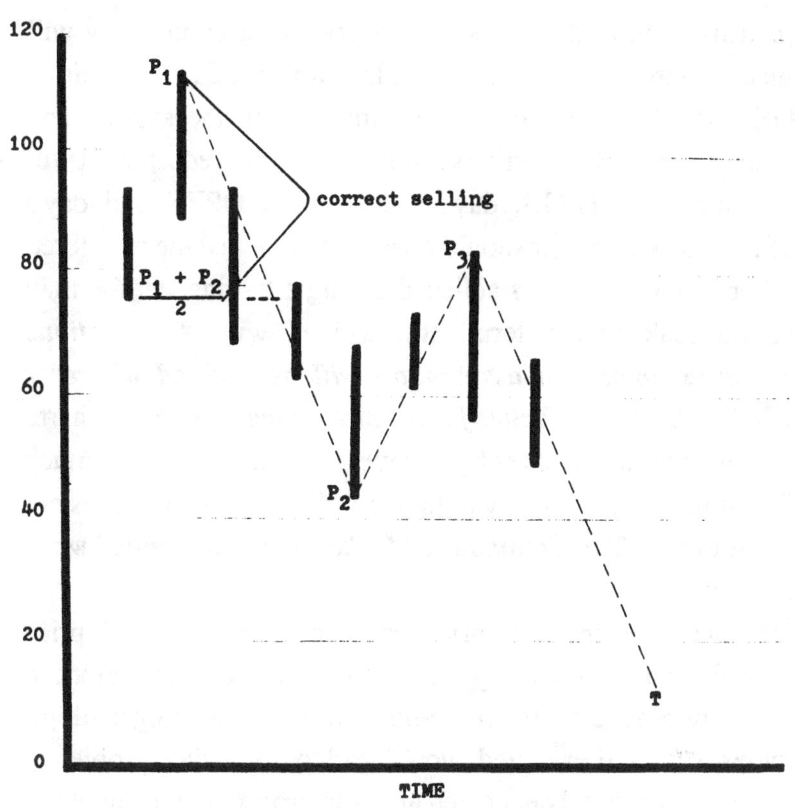


Figure 17. Correct Selling Region

During each trading session, the price of a commodity will fluctuate, establishing a high and a low for that day. The day's "HIGH OR LOW" can occur any time during the session and without warning. Most commodity price recording equipment will register the day's HIGH, day's LOW, day's OPEN and day's CLOSE. The wise trader should always assume that the registered HIGH or LOW thus far established during a trading session may well be the peak or valley terminating a given swing. ***Calculations made based upon that assumption will be verified wherever "ENTRY PRICE" is reached for the next swing.*** There is no harm calculating a trade whose entry is never reached. However, much profit can be lost if the entry point is reached and the trader is not prepared to act. ***The Commodity Market, just like "time," waits for no man.***

When calculating entry prices, make certain that the sell price is below P3 and that the buy price is above P3 . Some experienced Trident traders have made simple-minded errors resulting in illogical trades, which, if executed, would lead to immediate problems! Once a trade is properly executed and is in progress, the only thing to do next is manage that trade to a satisfactory conclusion.

The price of a Commodity Option (Contract) can be described as "Rising" or "Falling" depending upon which side of the market the best trading opportunity exists. If upon each price swing peaks and valleys move higher then the commodity price is "Rising." If, however, the opposite is true, then the commodity price is "Falling" (Figure 18). The problem with rising markets is that they eventually turn into falling markets and vice versa. (According to wave theory expounded by many researchers since the 40's, no more than five (5) swings in the same direction will occur without at least two (2) waves in an opposite direction — and there seems to be excellent evidence that this is correct.

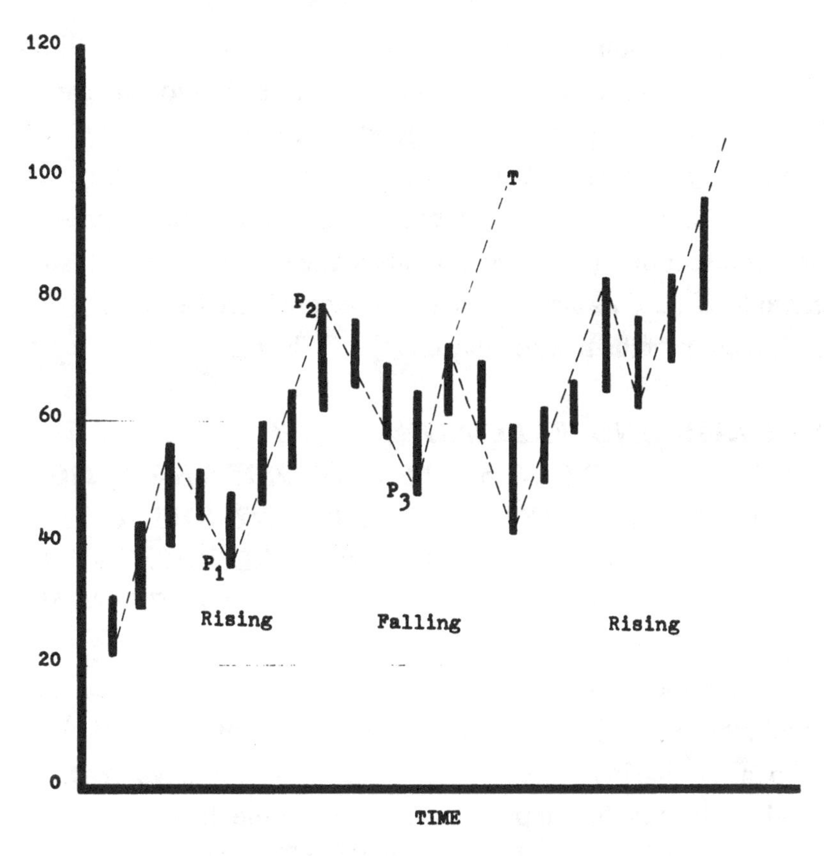


Figure 18. Rising vs Falling Market

Because commodity prices change from Rising to Falling without apparent warning, a strategy is required to protect against the risk that what appeared to be good tradeable action turned out to be merely the reaction before new action in an opposite direction. It is CRITICAL, therefore, that each trade guard against change in market direction. (Note: Many times a reaction swing will substantially exceed its target, which can be considered a warning that the direction of the market may change.) The rule to remember is:

***"IF IN A RISING (FALLING) MARKET, THE CURRENT ACTION SWING FAILS TO ESTABLISH A NEW HIGH (LOW) PRICE, THEN THE CURRENT SWING IS A REACTION SWING AND THE PREVIOUS SWING WAS THE FIRST ACTION SWING IN A NEW DIRECTION."***

Since the transition in market direction can occur on any swing, it is important to consider where this event is most likely to happen. Notice in Figure 18 that the target "T" was never reached, but the price reached approximately 50% of the distance P3 to T. The price level, 50% of the distance, P3 to T, is the most probable level at which a swing is likely to fail.

This price is called the CRITICAL PRICE because the success of a trade is dependent upon how well the price can penetrate this retracement area and break through to establish a new high or low. The ***CRITICAL PRICE,*** i.e., the price at which an expected price swing may fail, can be calculated as follows:

$$CP = \frac{P3 + T}{2} \qquad (3)$$

## STOPS, STOP DIFFERENTIAL

Commodity traders, experienced and inexperienced, enter trades with great expectation of making a profit, but haunted by the possibility that loss may occur. Most commodity textbooks suggest that a trader can expect to lose more often than win. The idea is that many small losses can be easily overcome by one big gain. This idea has little merit because the average commodity trader would have lost his initial capital waiting for that one big gain to wipe out his losses; and most traders do get wiped out just that way. The better idea, it seems, is to make trading profits more often than losing trade capital. Or, to be more specific, make profit on a trade even though the trade was wrong!

***MARKET LOSSES ARE INEVITABLE,*** however, losses can be cut to a minimum through the disciplined use of Protective Stops. The cardinal rule is:

***"THE MARKET IS TO MAKE MONEY, NOT TO PROVE WHO'S RIGHT OR WRONG."***

There is no such thing as right or wrong in the Commodity Market, there is only trades which succeed or fail. The Trident Trading Strategy is designed to put the odds for success in favor of the "TRIDENT TRADER" and not in chance. Failure is always tough on the ego, but it is better to trust objective pre-set rules than to worry about being right or wrong.

***PROTECTIVE STOPS*** are used to prevent large losses of capital should a trade go against the trader. Such stops are established in advance and represent the trader's judgement relative to when a losing trade should be abandoned. Overcoming the emotional impact of being stopped out of the market is perhaps the single greatest lesson to learn.

The Trident model reflects the emotional character of its creator, especially as regards to ***PROTECTIVE STOPS.*** Trident Trades should flow towards profit in harmony with the flow of price swings in the market. Price swings represent, generally, action or reaction. Each trade is based upon an action swing and the assumptive identification thereof. The moment the price action of the market proves the assumption false, the trade must be abandoned (stopped out).

Trident trades based upon establishment of P3 through 25% retracement (entry) assume P3 to be valid. If the Critical Price (CP) is not reached before P3 is penetrated, then the trade is invalid and should be stopped out (Figure 19 or 20). The specific rule for Protective Stops is as follows:

***"A TRIDENT TRADE ONCE EXECUTED MUST BE ABANDONED WHEN, AND IF, THE PRICE SWINGS ONE TICK BEYOND THE ESTABLISHED P3 ."***

One tick beyond P3 means exactly that. In a rising market (Figure 19), a new P3 is being formed the moment the price moves one tick below P3 . In a falling market (Figure 20), a new P3 is being formed the moment the price moves one tick above P3 . (The frequency of this occurrence is minimized through rules defining P3 qualification.)

## CHANGING PROTECTIVE STOPS

Protective Stops need not remain fixed. The initial Protective Stop is designed to protect against a loss of capital because the P3

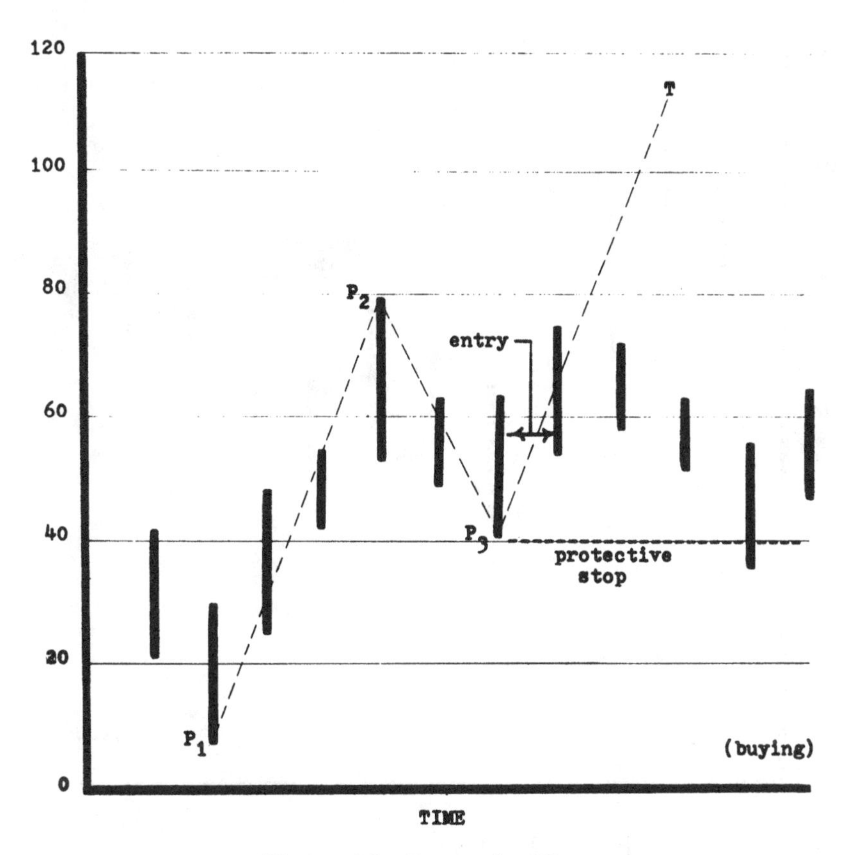


Figure 19. Protective Stops

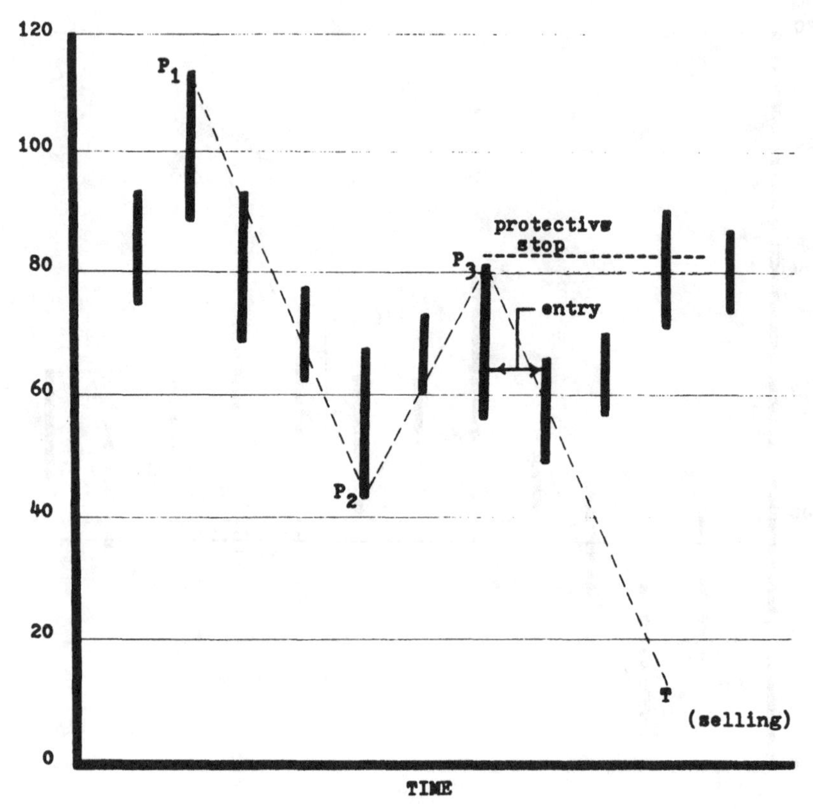


Figure 20. Protective Stops

basis of a trade proved invalid. Once a trade has progressed to the ***Critical Price,*** however, there is a degree of profit in the trade. A tentatively profitable trade no longer need carry the risk of loss, since the basis for that trade was valid. (Some Trident traders are quick to take profit at the Critical Price, and have indicated that Critical Price profit is available more than 85% of the time.)

Reaching the Critical Price is assumptive proof that P3 is valid and that the price swing will continue its action, or the market will change its trend direction. In either case, Protective Stops should be moved to ***Entry Price*** to guard against market trend changes. Using the ***Critical Price*** as a signal to change Protective Stops has the advantage of relieving anxiety concerning a particular trade. (Some traders feel enormous tension if a trade is in doubt.)

## STOP DIFFERENTIAL

A market rises by making higher highs followed by higher lows. Conversely, a market fails by making lower lows followed by lower highs. Market trends, once established, are assumed to continue until proven otherwise. Trident trades of action price swings expect the market to establish higher highs (Figure 21) or lower lows (Figure 22) depending upon the direction of the trade. The unique problem is, however, once a new high is made in a rising market (or new low in a falling market) the basic trend condition has been satisfied and the price can dip (or rally) without warning.

The Trident Trading Strategy takes into account the abrupt reversal possibility by defining "THE WINDOW." The Window is a price region one tick beyond P2 and extending to the Trident ideal target. Once the price swings into the Window, Protective Stops are lifted and replaced by a unique Trailing Stop.

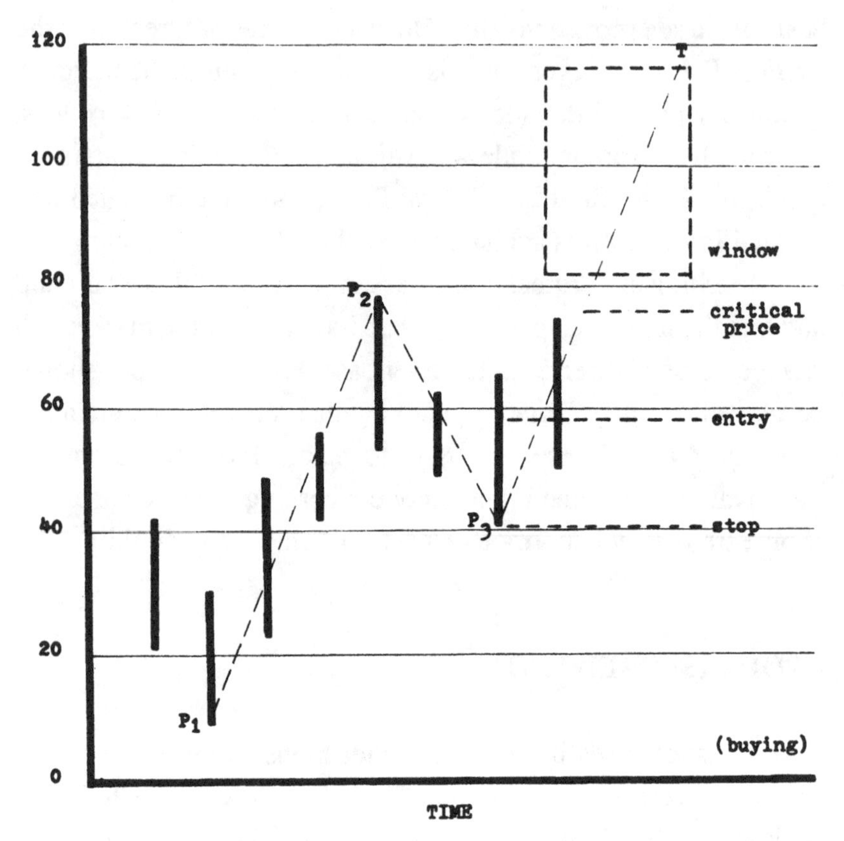


Figure 21. Trade Sequence

Assumptive evidence that a reaction swing has started is a reversal equal to 25% of the last reaction swing. Since the swing $P_2$ to $P_3$ (Figure 21) was the last reaction swing, then $(P_3 - P_2)/4$ would be 25% of that swing. Therefore the rule follows:

***"ONCE A TRADE HAS ENTERED THE WINDOW, A REVERSAL EQUAL TO $(P_3 - P_2)/4$ SIGNALS THE COMPLETION OF THAT TRADE."***

The reversal magnitude $(P_3 - P_2)/4$ is called the ***"STOP DIFFERENTIAL"*** and should be calculated in advance. The ***STOP DIFFERENTIAL*** once applied will insure profit, while at the same time, remedy many trading problems due to greed. ***ONCE THE STOP DIFFERENTIAL IS APPLIED AS A TRAILING STOP, AND THE TARGET IS REACHED BEFORE BEING STOPPED OUT (with profit), EXIT (offset trade) AT THE TRIDENT TARGET.***

$$\text{STOP DIFFERENTIAL} = \frac{P_3 - P_2}{4} \qquad (4)$$

## PROFIT vs RISK

The ***Profit*** in a Trident trade is always evaluated as potential profit. Potential Profit is measured from Entry Price to Target, applying the appropriate value of that move. Potential Profit should be evaluated before making a trade to determine if the trade is worthy of attention.

***Risk*** in a Trident trade is always evaluated as potential minimum Risk. Potential minimum risk is measured from Entry to $P_3$,

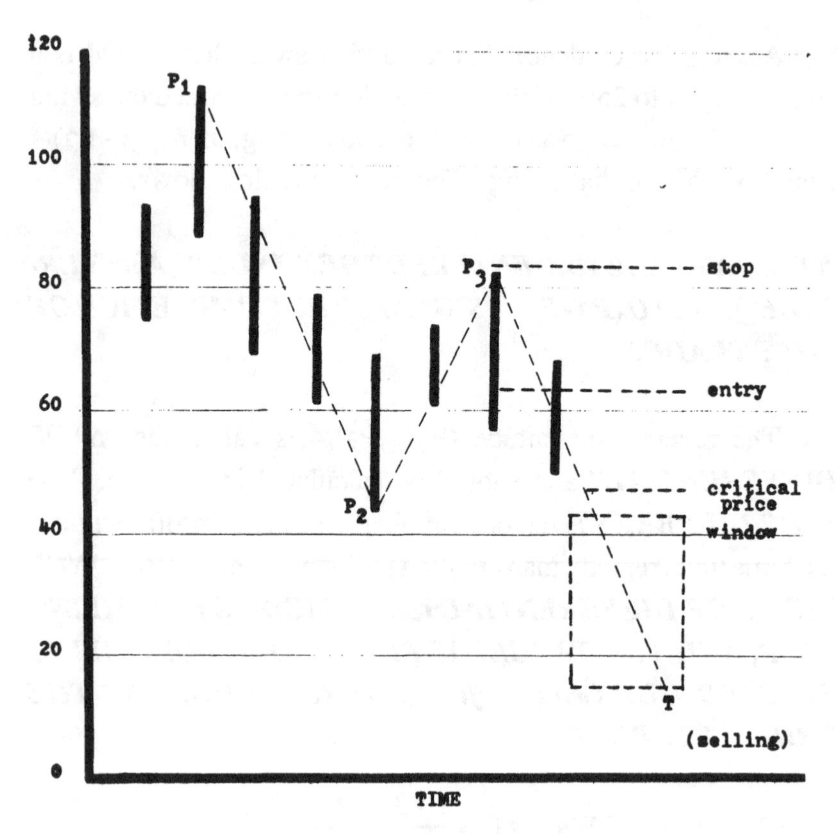


Figure 22. Trade Sequence

applying the value of that move. The ratio of Profit to Risk will always be 3 to 1, which is definitely in the trader's favor.

## THE TRIDENT

The Trident P1, P2, P3 represents a great wealth of information for trading purposes. Through application of a few simple equations, a trader can determine, in advance, sufficient information to control trade execution, management and completion (more information than the average trader uses). The Trident contains information concerning market phase (Action or Reaction) as well as market trend (Rising or Falling). The great wealth of information contained within the Trident gives a trading advantage that could protect a trader from loss of capital caused through lack of awareness. Trident information provides the trader with an objective criteria, although assumptive, which supports personal confidence and promotes rational trading habits.

## TRIDENT INFORMATION LINE

***THE TRIDENT TRADING STRATEGY*** requires accurate data preparation and layout in order to insure positive trading results (Figure 24). A worksheet should be prepared in advance and trade decisions made in light of the fully detailed information. The worksheet information, once recorded, becomes a convenient reminder of the trade **BASIS, OBJECTIVES, STOPS** and more. The few minutes required to calculate and record the Trident Information Line will save both time and money, when and if a trade is executed.

Trading Trident successfully is a matter of practice, because practice makes perfect, and making money **(PROFIT)** is the only reason for trading commodities. The Trident model exists as a theoretical tool whose only value lies in its application to the **REAL MARKET.** How the tool is applied is a matter of personal character, but should Trident be applied seriously, accurately and objectively, significant profit with reduced risk is available on a daily basis.

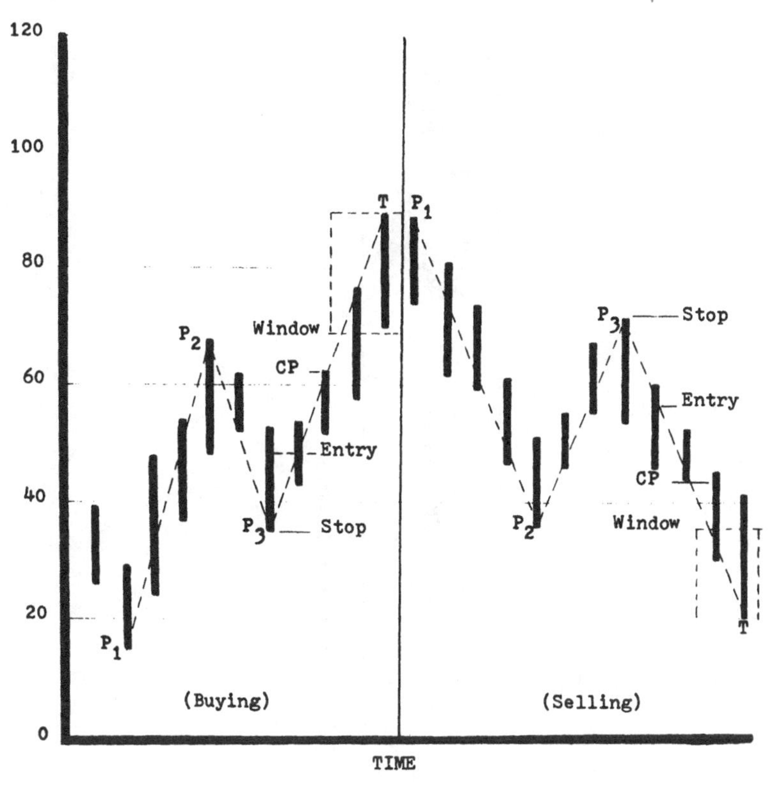


Figure 23. Trident Price Swing Model

| TRIDENT PRICES | | | TARGET PRICE | CRITICAL PRICE | ENTRY PRICE | PROFIT AMOUNT | STOP PROTECTED | STOP DIFFERENTIAL | RISK AMOUNT |
|---|---|---|---|---|---|---|---|---|---|
| $P_1$ | $P_2$ | $P_3$ | | | | | | | |
| xxx.xx | xxx.xx | xxx.xx | xxx.xx | xxx.x | xxx.xx | xxx.xx | xxx.xx | xxx.xx | xxx.xx |

Figure 24. Trident Worksheet

# TRIDENT MARKET APPLICATIONS

# CHAPTER 4

Trading the Commodity Market using Trident Strategy is probably one of the most exciting pleasures ever experienced by a Commodity Trader on an ongoing basis. Watching commodity prices confirm, time and again, the basic Trident assumptions must be experienced in order to appreciate the incredible symmetry of price action exhibited by the market. Observing Trident formations and having trades executed at the proper moment and then seeing the price accelerate toward the Critical Price and beyond, is an experience reserved for those traders who take the time to master this strategy.

***EACH TRIDENT TRADE DISCUSSED IN THIS CHAPTER IS TAKEN FROM REAL-MARKET ACTUAL TRADES AND REFLECTS THE COMMON EXPERIENCE OF NUMEROUS TRIDENT USERS.***

There are four (4) steps involved in trading Trident:

***DATA COLLECTION***
***TRIDENT CALCULATIONS***
***BROKER ORDERS***
***TRADE MANAGEMENT***

Each step is necessary in order to complete the trading cycle. The four (4) steps taken as a whole represent the complete Trident Trading System.

## DATA COLLECTION

Price data (Table 2) is available through many sources depending upon trader convenience. However, price data ***MUST BE CURRENT*** (i.e., arrangements must be made to obtain price data after the close of market and before the market opens the next day). Many traders use local newspapers, the Wall Street Journal, check with their broker, or use a data quote service.

The ***wise and prudent*** Commodity Trader will make certain that the source of price data is reasonably accurate, or at least has a history of reliability. As a matter of fact, hundreds of dollars hinge upon trading decisions solely dependent upon the reliability of data collected.

Price data should be maintained in a particular sequence (Table 2). Any standard paper (8 ½ x 11) is suitable for data collection. Separate columns should be maintained for **DATE-OPEN-HIGH-LOW-CLOSE.** The opening and closing prices are very important in order to determine the sequence of price events during the trading session. If, for example, the market opens high and closes low, then the likelihood is that the high of the day was made prior to the low of the day. The importance of this sequence will become apparent when the minor high and the minor low occur on the same day.

Price data analysis is a simple procedure. The single purpose of price data analysis is to identify price swings within the same level (Minor, Intermediate, Major). The procedure is called ringing. A ringed high or a ringed low is simply the Trident price $P_1$, $P_2$, $P_3$ . . . etc. . . . used exclusively for Trident calculations. The ringing procedure is as follows:

1. Starting in the daily price high column, locate a daily high

Commodity: *CATTLE AUGUST 1975*

| DATE | OPEN | HIGH | LOW | CLOSE |
|---|---|---|---|---|
| 6/20/75 | 50.00 | 50.60 | 49.70 | 50.22 |
| 6/23/75 | 50.25 | (50.65) | 49.97 | 50.05 |
| 6/24/75 | 49.90 | 50.25 | 49.35 | 49.47 |
| 6/25/75 | 49.55 | 49.77 | 48.00 | 48.07 |
| 6/26/75 | 47.75 | 48.95 | (47.40) | 48.30 |
| 6/27/75 | 48.50 | 48.80 | 47.50 | 47.70 |
| 6/30/75 | 47.74 | (48.85) | 47.45 | 48.70 |
| 7/01/75 | 48.60 | 48.60 | 47.20 | 47.20 |

Table 2. Price Data

which is higher than the previous day's high and higher than the following day's high. Enclose this price in parentheses.

2. In the column for daily price lows identify the next low after the ring high, which is lower than the previous day's low and is lower than the following day's low. Enclose this price in parentheses.

3. Repeat steps 1 and 2, alternating between the daily high and daily low columns, until all the price data has been analyzed.

(Many Trident students use a blue pencil or pen to ring the daily high price column and red pen or pencil to ring the daily low price column.)

The price data (Table 2) has been ringed, identifying a daily price high (50.65) followed by the low (47.40) and the next high (48.85). Ringing identifies price swings without the need for graphs. Properly ringed price data reveals considerable information about the commodity within a glance. The trader can determine trend direction, action-reaction swings and trend reversals.

Once minor price swings have been identified through the ringing process, higher level swings must be considered. Intermediate highs and lows (highest minor high or lowest minor low) are ringed following the same procedure; steps 1 through 3 above. The result is a double ring high or low. Likewise, the highest Intermediate high and the lowest Intermediate low form major ringed highs and lows. The result is a triple ringed high or low, forming major price swings (it is suggested that the student now practice ringing price data using daily price data obtained from reliable sources).

## TRIDENT CALCULATIONS

Based upon the data collected (Table 2) the following price swings are determined:

$$P_1, 50.65 \quad P_2, 47.40 \quad P_3, 48.85$$

Simple inspection reveals that the trend is down (Falling Market) because $P_3$ is below $P_1$, and the action is therefore on the short (Sell) side of the market. Therefore, the best opportunity for profit will come from selling the commodity. The following calculations are made:

*TARGET:*

$$\begin{aligned} T &= P_2 + P_3 - P_1 \\ &= 47.40 + 48.85 - 50.65 \\ &= 96.25 - 50.65 \\ &\equiv \underline{45.60} \end{aligned}$$

*CRITICAL PRICE:*

$$\begin{aligned} CP &= (P_3 + T) + 2 \\ &= (48.85 + 45.60) + 2 \\ &= 94.45 + 2 \\ &\equiv \underline{47.23} \end{aligned}$$

*ENTRY:*

$$\begin{aligned} EP &= (P_2 - P_1) + 4 + P_3 \\ &= (47.40 - 50.65) + 4 + 48.85 \\ &= -3.25 + 4 + 48.85 \\ &= -.81 + 48.85 \\ &\equiv \underline{48.04} \end{aligned}$$

| | | | | | | |
|---|---|---|---|---|---|---|
| *PROFIT:* | = (E.P. | - | T) | x | 1¢ | Value |
| | = (48.04 | - | 45.60) | x | \$400 | |
| | = 2.44 | | | x | \$400 | |
| | ≡ <u>\$976.00</u> | | | | | |

| | | | |
|---|---|---|---|
| *STOP:* | = $P_3$ | + | TICK |
| | = 48.85 | + | .02 |
| | ≡ <u>48.87</u> | | |

| | | | | | |
|---|---|---|---|---|---|
| *STOP DIFFERENTIAL:* | = ($P_3$ | - | $P_2$) | ÷ | 4 |
| | = (48.85 | - | 47.40) | ÷ | 4 |
| | = 1.45 | | | | |
| | ≡ <u>.36</u> | | | | |

| | | | | | | |
|---|---|---|---|---|---|---|
| *RISK:* | = ($P_3$ | - | EP) | x | 1¢ | Value |
| | = (48.85 | - | 48.04) | x | \$400 | |
| | = .81 | | | x | \$400 | |
| | ≡ <u>\$324.00</u> | | | | | |

EACH CALCULATION IS RECORDED ON THE WORKSHEET (See Table 3a).

The Chart (Figure 25) illustrates the results of the calculations. Observe the automatic forecast and trade sequence from formation of $P_3$, Entry, Critical Price through Target. (The average trader uses far less information and thus invites surprises.)

| TRIDENT PRICES | | | TARGET PRICE | CRITICAL PRICE | ENTRY PRICE | PROFIT AMOUNT | STOP PROTECTED | STOP DIFFERENTIAL | RISK AMOUNT |
|---|---|---|---|---|---|---|---|---|---|
| $P_1$ | $P_2$ | $P_3$ | | | | | | | |
| 50.65 | 47.40 | 48.85 | 45.60 | 47.23 | 48.04 | $976.00 | 48.87 | .36 | $324.00 |

Table 3a. Trident Information Line

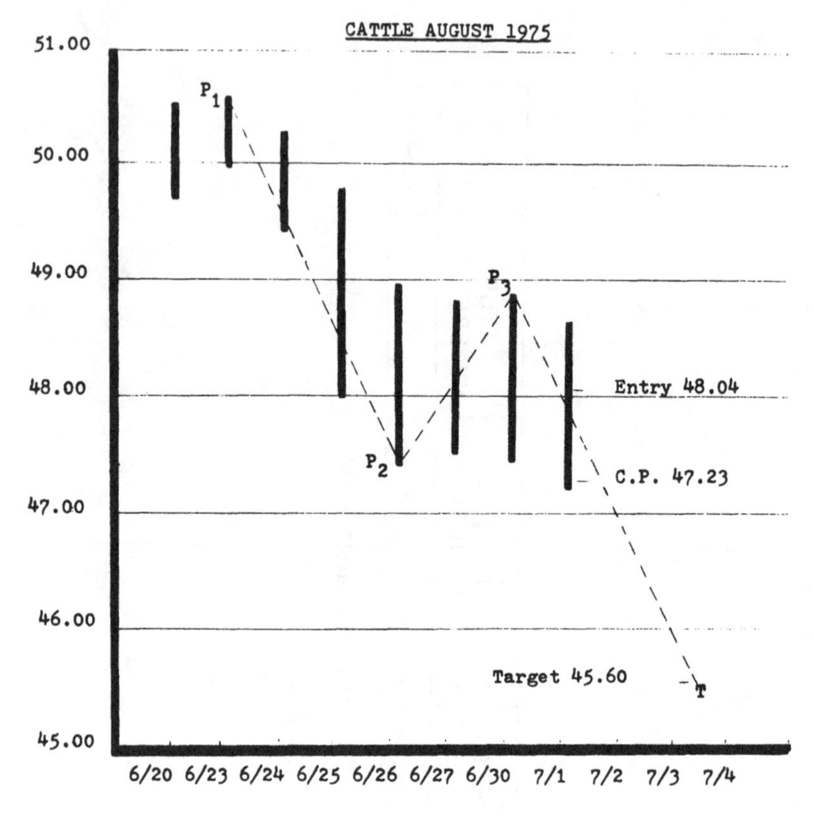


Figure 25. Price Data Chart

## BROKER ORDERS

The order to the Commodity Broker is simple and straight forward:

| | |
|---|---|
| ***SELL STOP AUGUST CATTLE*** | 48.03 |
| ***PLACE PROTECTIVE STOP*** | 48.87 |
| ***OBJECTIVE*** | 45.60 |

The broker then places this order with the Chicago Mercantile Exchange with his Floor Broker. Specifically, this order means:

***SELL ONE AUGUST CATTLE CONTRACT WHEN AND IF THE PRICE MOVES DOWN TO 48.03. IF THE TRADE IS EXECUTED, RECORD AN ORDER TO BUY ONE AUGUST CATTLE CONTRACT WHEN AND IF THE PRICE SHOULD RISE TO 48.87 OR HIGHER (PROTECTIVE STOP); AND, RECORD AN ORDER TO BUY ONE AUGUST CATTLE CONTRACT WHEN AND IF THE PRICE MOVES DOWN TO 45.60 OR LOWER (OBJECTIVE).***

Once the order is placed with the Floor Broker (by your broker) the sequence of events is automatic from the traders standpoint. (In the case of this actual trade, the order was placed at 7:55 a.m., Tuesday, July 1st, 1975 and executed 8:15 a.m., 20 minutes later.)

## TRADE MANAGEMENT

A Trident Trade, once executed, must be managed by the trader (or the broker, if proper arrangements can be made) as the trade progresses through the Critical Price, and/or Window, whichever occurs first. In this specific case, the Window (47.37) occurs before the Critical Price (47.23). However, either could have occurred before the other.

During the trading session (8:50 a.m.), the price of August Cattle moved into the Window (47.37), which required application of the Stop Differential (.36) as a Trailing Stop to protect profits made thus far. A new instruction must be given to the broker:

***AUGUST CATTLE:***
***CANCEL PROTECTIVE STOP 48.87;***
***OFFSET TRADE UPON ANY RALLY OF 36***
***POINTS FROM THE LOWEST PRICE REACHED.***

This instruction means that the trade will be offset (buy back the contract previously sold) should the price move up 36 points. At the same time this instruction is given, the price of August Cattle is at 47.37 (thereabout) and the maximum Offset Price would be:

WINDOW + STOP DIFFERENTIAL, OR
$47.37 + .36 = 47.73$;

locking in a minimum profit of $48.04 - 47.73 = 31$ points or $124.00.

The four (4) steps detailed above are typical of Trident Trading. In the actual trade, the sequence of events was as follows:

***JULY 1, 1975***

7:55 a.m. — Original order (price of August Cattle was 48.30)
Sell August Cattle 48.03, Protective Stop 48.87.
Objective 45.60

8:15 a.m. — Order executed.
Sell Price reached 48.03.

8:50 a.m. — Window reached.
Price of Cattle had moved below 47.40 (P2).

10:45 a.m. — Close
Cattle had reached limit down (47.20) and remained there.

***JULY 2, 1975***

7:25 a.m. — Cattle opened.
Price of Cattle was at 46.25.

7:55 a.m. — Stopped out.
Cattle had rallied 36 points.
Actual Offset Price 46.63.
Profit $560.00

***JULY 7, 1975***

7:15 a.m. — New P3 formed.
Cattle reached a high of 47.75 on opening.
Never moved below 46.25.

8:16 a.m. — New trade advised. Sell Stop August Cattle 47.10.
Place Protective Stop 47.77 Objective 45.15.

9:00 a.m. — Entry reached (47.10).

10:45 a.m. — Market closed at 46.90

***JULY 8, 1975***

7:15 a.m. — Market opened at 45.40.

Stop Differential of 37 points applied.
7:30 a.m. — Stopped out 45.77
Profit $532.00
Both trades realized **$1,092.00 Profit.**

The Commodity Trading environment is filled with unexpected events for the average trader. Unexpected events occur frequently because too many trades are made for emotional reasons. The fact that the market holds many surprises for traders is not very mysterious, considering the fluctuating natural swing motion of Commodity Price Action.

The Trident Trading environment is substantially different from the surprised-filled, emotional (sometimes irrational), and game-oriented trading experienced by the average non-Trident Trader. There are, for example, five (5) unique outcomes possible in a Trident Trade. The five (5) possibilities are:

1. Trade Entry not reached.
2. Trade stopped out with loss (RISK).
3. Trade stopped out at Entry.
4. Trade stopped out by Stop Differential.
5. Trade offset at Target.

Each of the five (5) possibilities can and do occur. However, tacit Trident assumptions favor the latter three (3) outcomes. It is significant that of the five (5) outcome possibilities, three (3) are positive (PROFIT), one is neutral, while only one is negative. This means that Trident Trading odds are at least 3 to 1 in favor of the trader. And actually are substantially better!

The following examples are selected from real time trades and will illustrate the five (5) possible Trident Trade outcomes.

## TRADE ENTRY NOT REACHED

The Trident Trading Strategy requires the trader to be constantly on the lookout for formation of the next peak or valley (P3). Because many levels of price swing action occur simultaneously in the market, subordinate price swings create the illusion of a potentially tradeable swing within the swing level desired. The results of subordinate swing activity may be several false starts before an actual Trident Trade is executed.

Failure to reach the Entry Price of a Trident Trade creates no financial consequences, and therefore, does not represent a serious trading concern. With practice, the frequency of false starts will be greatly reduced, primarily because experience is gained towards recognizing the logical price regions for P3 formation. Nevertheless, false starts are certain and true evidence that the trader is on the right track. Ultimately, a trade will result.

## TRADE STOPPED OUT WITH LOSS (RISK)

The Trident Trading Strategy does not exclude the possibility of market losses. The statistical odds are 1 in 5 that a given trade will result in a modest loss. Making trade profits is not dependent upon improving the statistical odds against losses, but rather the consistent application of the Trident Strategy. This fact is reinforced over many Trident Trades which point to a track record of better than 80% profit retention.

Experienced Trident Traders have observed that although some losses are unavoidable, still others can be avoided through analysis of price swings at the next higher level. In general, the Target of a higher level trade has priority over the Target of a subordinate level price swing. Inter-level Target conflict frequently happens when $P_2$ represents a peak or valley culminating a higher level price swing. The losing trade results from trading a first reaction leg of a trend change, mistaking that swing for a valid tradeable action. To illustrate this point, consider the following example (Table 3).

## DATA COLLECTION

$P_1$ (3.77 ½), and $P_2$ (3.48) are well established. However, P3 must be selected shortly after the market opens on 7/16. The Intermediate Target was 4.24 $I_1$ (3.01 ½), $I_2$ (3.77 ½), $I_3$ (3.48); the Intermediate Critical Price was 3.86. Twenty minutes after the opening of the market (on 7/16), the price of Wheat established an inter-day high of 3.73 and began to decline from that price level. An order was given for a possible Trident Trade:

***SELL STOP SEPT WHEAT*** ***3.65 ¾***
***PLACE PROTECTIVE STOP*** ***3.73 ¼***
***SELL STOP SEPT WHEAT*** ***3.43 ½***

Twenty-five minutes later a trade was executed and immediately the price began to move against the trade, resulting in being stopped out at 3.73 ¼ with a loss of $369.00

Comparing the Information Line for the Minor Trade (Table 4), with the Information Line for the Intermediate Trade (Table 5), indicates logical conflict between the Intermediate and Minor Targets. The Target for the Minor Trade is pointing down, while the Target for the Intermediate Trade is pointing up; whenever such conflicts exist, resolution must be in favor of the more dominant

Commodity: *WHEAT SEPT 1975*

| DATE | OPEN | HIGH | LOW | CLOSE |
|---|---|---|---|---|
| 7/03/75 | 3.02½ | 3.11½ | (3.02½) | 3.06 |
| 7/07/75 | 3.08 | 3.15 | 3.08 | 3.08½ |
| 7/08/75 | 3.10 | 3.28¼ | 3.10 | 3.28¼ |
| 7/09/75 | 3.33½ | 3.43½ | 3.26½ | 3.39 |
| 7/10/75 | 3.41 | 3.58½ | 3.39 | 3.50 |
| 7/11/75 | 3.53 | 3.70 | 3.52 | 3.65 |
| 7/14/75 | 3.67½ | (3.77½) | 3.56 | 3.58 |
| 7/15/75 | 3.54 | 3.70 | (3.48) | 3.63 |
| 7/16/75 | 3.68 | 3.80 | 3.65 | 3.78 |
| 7/17/75 | 3.83 | (3.84) | 3.62 | 3.64 |
| 7/18/75 | 3.60 | 3.64 | 3.51 | 3.51 |

Table 3. WHEAT Prices

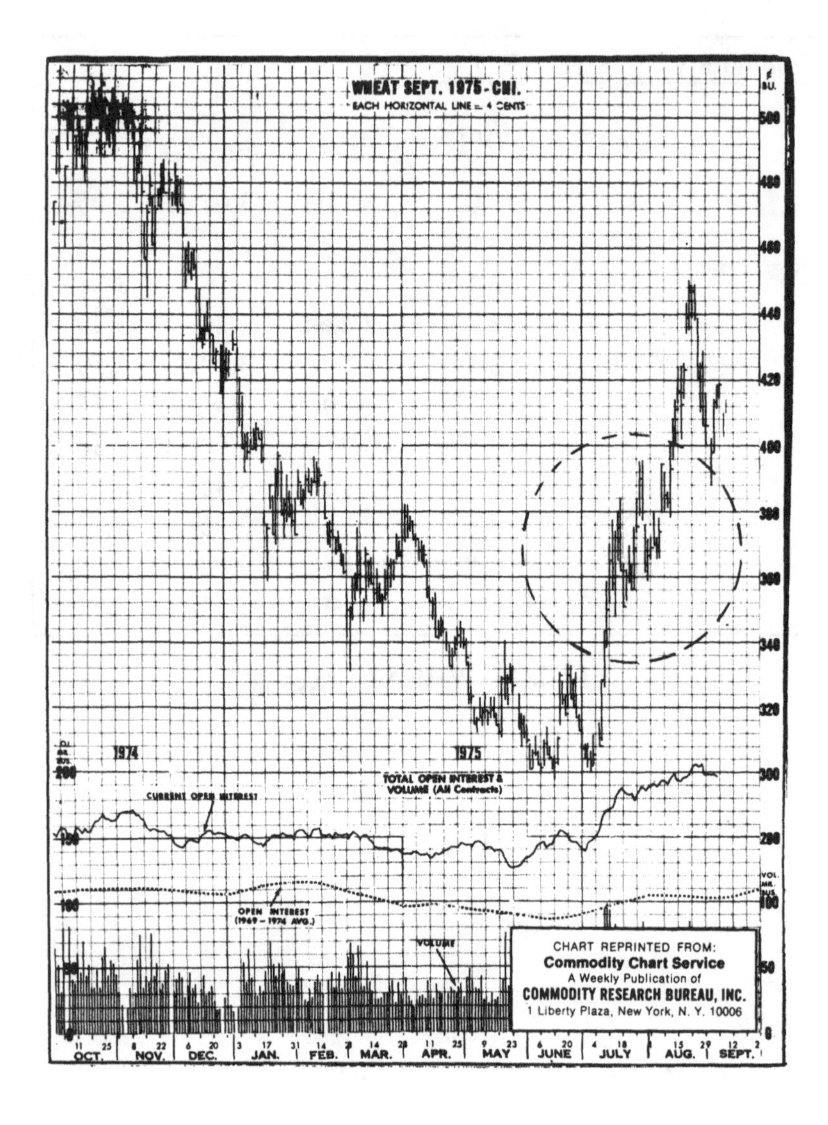
WHEAT SEPT. 1975 - CHI.
EACH HORIZONTAL LINE = 4 CENTS
¢ BU.
500
480
460
440
420
400
380
360
340
320
300
280
1974
1975
CURRENT OPEN INTEREST
TOTAL OPEN INTEREST & VOLUME (All Contracts)
OPEN INTEREST (1969 – 1974 AVG.)
VOLUME
VOL. MIL. BUS.
100
50
0
CHART REPRINTED FROM:
Commodity Chart Service
A Weekly Publication of
COMMODITY RESEARCH BUREAU, INC.
1 Liberty Plaza, New York, N. Y. 10006
OCT.
NOV.
DEC.
JAN.
FEB.
MAR.
APR.
MAY
JUNE
JULY
AUG.
SEPT.

| TRIDENT PRICES | | | TARGET PRICE | CRITICAL PRICE | ENTRY PRICE | PROFIT AMOUNT | STOP PROTECTED | STOP DIFFERENTIAL | RISK AMOUNT |
|---|---|---|---|---|---|---|---|---|---|
| $P_1$ | $P_2$ | $P_3$ | | | | | | | |
| 3.775 | 3.480 | 3.730 | 3.535 | 3.582 | 3.656 | $1,106. | 3.731 | 6.25 | $373.01 |

Table 4. Trident Information Line — WHEAT TRADE

| TRIDENT PRICES | | | TARGET PRICE | CRITICAL PRICE | ENTRY PRICE | PROFIT AMOUNT | STOP PROTECTED | STOP DIFFERENTIAL | RISK AMOUNT |
|---|---|---|---|---|---|---|---|---|---|
| $I_1$ | $I_2$ | $I_3$ | | | | | | | |
| 3.01½ | 3.77½ | 3.48 | 4.24 | 3.86 | 3.67 | $2,850. | 3.47¾ | 7.4¢ | $950.00 |

Table 5. Trident Information Line — INTERMEDIATE WHEAT TRADE

price swing level. Specifically, ***the Intermediate move has priority over the Minor move.*** Had this rule been applied, the loss of $369.00 could have been avoided.

## TRADE STOPPED OUT AT ENTRY

The Critical Price is the first milestone of a Trident Trade. Once a trade has been executed (off and running), "No Man's Land" (price region between Entry and Critical Price), is immediately encountered. Fortunately, most Trident Trades negotiate this price region rapidly, depending upon which trade level price swing is being traded. Penetration of the Critical Price is an event which signals significant risk reduction because protective stops are moved to the Entry Price. The original risk (statistical) remains with the trade until the Critical Price is reached. The market, rather than the Trident Trader, is in control of the trade until the Critical Price is reached.

A Trident Trade which terminates by being stopped out at Entry is considered neutral. The theory behind changing protective stops after penetration of the Critical Price is: Good trades reach Entry once and only once (continuous swing) and therefore, there should be one best opportunity to enter that trade. Once a price swing has progressed 50% of its course, this is positive assumptive evidence that the trade decision was correct, and capital need not continue in jeopardy. ***(Students in Trident classes were taught to be suspicious of trades which give two or more opportunities to make profit: if the trade is really good, then what is it waiting for?)***

A price swing which fails to progress beyond the Critical Price is often a signal that the trend direction of that market has changed.

When this happens, the action-reaction swing cycle has reversed phases and the current trade is in a reaction, rather than good tradeable action. ***(Some Trident Traders trade only to the Critical Price, believing that a "Bird in the hand is worth the other two in the bush.")***

The following example illustrates a trade that was stopped out at Entry.

$P_1$ (4.20), $P_2$ (3.85 ¼), and $P_3$ (4.07 ½) are well established (Table 6). The Trident indicates that action is on the "downside," (market should work lower). The Trident Trader should always check the status of the Intermediate Trident before making a trade: in this case the Intermediate Trident $I_1$ (4.04), $I_2$ (3.74), $I_3$ (4.20) reveals that the market is in an Intermediate reaction phase and has completed (at least) one swing in the reaction direction. The Intermediate Target is (IT) 3.90. Applying the rule of price swing priority, (next higher level price swing takes priority) the Minor Trade Target (T) 3.72 ¾ should not be reached (Table 7).

It is significant that the Critical Price (CP) 3.90 is equal to the Intermediate Target (IT) 3.90. The Trident Trader must be constantly on the lookout for this type of situation because the Minor Trade is doomed to failure even though, on the surface, it appears to be a valid trade. (On 8/6/75 the Minor Trade was stopped out at Entry (3.98 ¾) after penetration of the Critical Price (3.90) only to rally up to 4.20 ½ the next day.)

## TRADE STOPPED OUT BY STOP DIFFERENTIAL

The Trident Trader can expect to be stopped out with profit by the applied Stop Differential more frequently than the other four (4) possible outcomes. Trident Ideal Targets are assumptive and

Commodity: *WHEAT MAR 1975*

| DATE | OPEN | HIGH | LOW | CLOSE |
|---|---|---|---|---|
| 7/16/75 | 3.89 | 3.94½ | 3.86 | 3.99 |
| 7/17/75 | 4.02 | ((4.04)) | 3.81½ | 3.86 |
| 7/18/75 | 3.82 | 3.84 | ((3.74)) | 3.76 |
| 7/21/75 | 3.80 | 3.85 | 3.77½ | 3.83 |
| 7/22/75 | 3.90 | 3.92¾ | 3.83 | 3.86 |
| 7/23/75 | 3.85 | 3.86½ | 3.79½ | 3.79½ |
| 7/24/75 | 3.80½ | 3.98½ | 3.80½ | 3.93½ |
| 7/25/75 | 3.99 | 4.07½ | 3.98½ | 4.00 |
| 7/28/75 | 4.08 | 4.19 | 4.04 | 4.14½ |
| 7/29/75 | 4.19 | ((4.20)) | 4.04 | 4.07 |
| 7/30/75 | 3.99 | 4.01 | 3.88 | 3.89 |
| 7/31/75 | 3.89 | 3.97 | (3.85¼) | 3.92 |
| 8/01/75 | 3.95 | 3.97 | 3.91 | 3.96 |
| 8/04/75 | 3.99 | (4.07½) | 3.96 | 3.98½ |
| 8/05/75 | 3.96 | 3.98 | 3.92½ | 3.95 |
| 8/06/75 | 3.95 | 4.04 | 3.89 | 4.00 |
| 8/07/75 | 4.11 | 4.20½ | 4.09½ | 4.20½ |

Table 6. MARCH WHEAT Prices

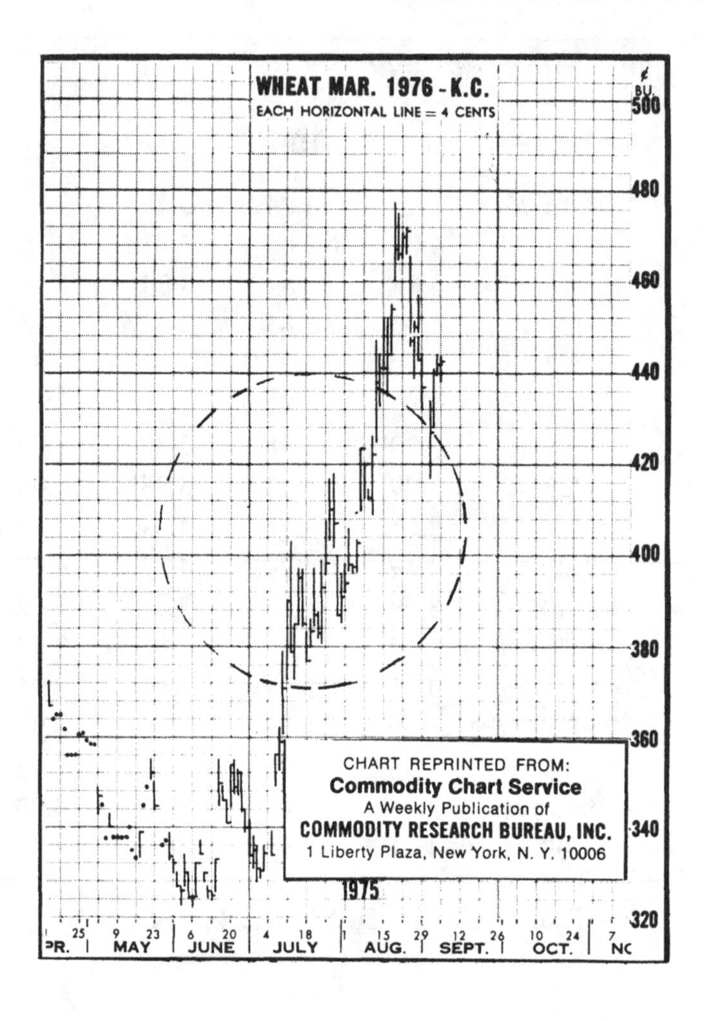
WHEAT MAR. 1976 - K.C.
EACH HORIZONTAL LINE = 4 CENTS
¢
BU.
500
480
460
440
420
400
380
360
340
320
CHART REPRINTED FROM:
Commodity Chart Service
A Weekly Publication of
COMMODITY RESEARCH BUREAU, INC.
1 Liberty Plaza, New York, N. Y. 10006
1975
25
9
23
6
20
4
18
1
15
29
12
26
10
24
7
PR.
MAY
JUNE
JULY
AUG.
SEPT.
OCT.
NC

| TRIDENT PRICES | | | TARGET PRICE | CRITICAL PRICE | ENTRY PRICE | PROFIT AMOUNT | STOP PROTECTED | STOP DIFFERENTIAL | RISK AMOUNT |
|---|---|---|---|---|---|---|---|---|---|
| $P_1$ | $P_2$ | $P_3$ | | | | | | | |
| 4.20 | 3.85¼ | 4.07½ | 3.72¾ | 3.90 | 3.98¾ | $1,300. | 4.07½ | 5.5¢ | $437.50 |

**Table 7. Minor Trade Information Line**

reflect directional ideas rather than predictive fact. The reason to trade commodities is to make money rather than accurately predict the future. Making money (Profits) is a matter of strategy, i.e. creating a statistical model of the market which includes basic rules and assumptions in accord with the way price-action occurs most often and most consistently.

The Stop Differential (Trailing Protective Stop), once applied to a Trident Trade in progress, is designed to protect trade profit, while at the same time acknowledge that a higher high or lower low is all the market need achieve prior to a trend reversal. Being stopped out with profit is a positive experience and should be regarded as such even when the price swing may subsequently reach the more profitable Target. (Some Trident Traders feel cheated when the Stop Differential causes premature profits if the Target is ultimately reached. Such an attitude is not consistent with the reality of making money.)

The following example illustrates a trade which was stopped out with a profit by the Stop Differential (see Table 8).

### *Trade Analysis*

Inspection of the Intermediate Trident $I_1$ (44.62), $I_2$ (51.70), and $I_3$ (47.05), (price data not shown) reveals an Intermediate action swing to the upside (IT = 54.13), which is well beyond the Minor Target (52.95) (Table 9). This trade can be expected to reach the Minor Target. However, the Window (51.77) must be considered and the Stop Differential (.70) applied.

An order was given 7:30 a.m., on 8/15:

Commodity: *HOGS DEC 1975*

| DATE | OPEN | HIGH | LOW | CLOSE |
|---|---|---|---|---|
| 8/01/75 | 48.55 | 49.30 | 47.05 | 48.37 |
| 8/04/75 | 48.10 | 49.55 | 47.70 | 48.12 |
| 8/05/75 | 47.77 | 48.65 | (47.40) | 48.57 |
| 8/06/75 | 48.15 | 48.95 | 47.95 | 48.87 |
| 8/07/75 | 49.32 | 50.37 | 49.25 | 50.32 |
| 8/08/75 | 50.42 | 50.45 | 49.50 | 49.67 |
| 8/11/75 | 50.30 | 50.92 | 50.10 | 50.70 |
| 8/12/75 | 50.35 | (51.75) | 49.77 | 50.22 |
| 8/13/75 | 50.42 | 50.70 | 49.30 | 49.37 |
| 8/14/75 | 49.32 | 49.50 | (48.60) | 49.00 |
| 8/15/75 | 48.92 | 50.50 | 48.80 | 50.47 |
| 8/18/75 | 50.30 | 50.90 | 49.75 | 50.15 |
| 8/19/75 | 50.37 | 51.15 | 50.05 | 51.10 |
| 8/20/75 | 51.35 | 52.00 | 51.02 | 51.70 |
| 8/21/75 | 51.95 | 52.75 | 51.40 | 52.30 |
| 8/22/75 | 52.55 | 53.82* | 52.55 | 53.82 |

Table 8. DEC HOGS Price Data

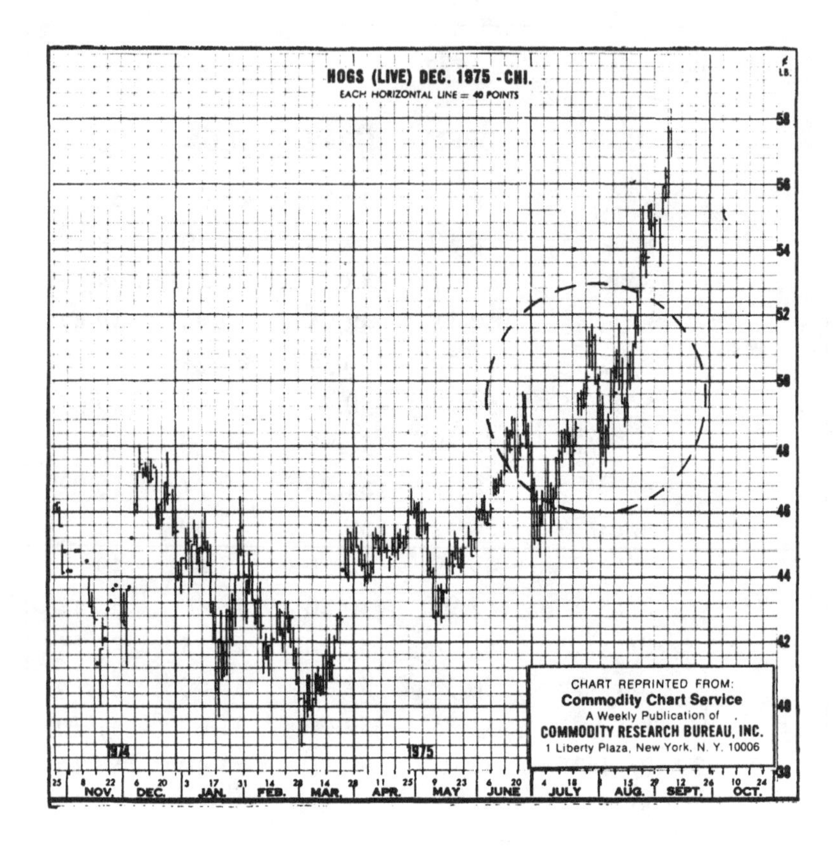
HOGS (LIVE) DEC. 1975 - CHI.
EACH HORIZONTAL LINE = 40 POINTS
¢ LB.
58
56
54
52
50
48
46
44
42
40
38
1974
1975
25 8 22 NOV. 6 20 DEC. 3 17 JAN. 31 14 FEB. 28 14 MAR. 28 11 25 APR. 9 23 MAY 6 20 JUNE 4 18 JULY 1 15 AUG. 29 12 SEPT. 26 10 24 OCT.
CHART REPRINTED FROM:
Commodity Chart Service
A Weekly Publication of
COMMODITY RESEARCH BUREAU, INC.
1 Liberty Plaza, New York, N. Y. 10006

| TRIDENT PRICES | | | TARGET PRICE | CRITICAL PRICE | ENTRY PRICE | PROFIT AMOUNT | STOP PROTECTED | STOP DIFFERENTIAL | RISK AMOUNT |
|---|---|---|---|---|---|---|---|---|---|
| $P_1$ | $P_2$ | $P_3$ | | | | | | | |
| 47.40 | 51.75 | 48.60 | 52.95 | 50.77 | 49.70 | $975.00 | 48.57 | .79 | $327.00 |

Table 9. Trident Information Line — HOG TRADE

Commodity: *CATTLE DEC 1975*

| DATE | OPEN | HIGH | LOW | CLOSES |
|---|---|---|---|---|
| 7/03/75 | 39.45 | 40.35 | (39.35) | 40.10 |
| 7/07/75 | 40.32 | (40.77) | 39.35 | 39.50 |
| 7/08/75 | 38.95 | 39.85 | ((38.25)) | 39.05 |
| 7/09/75 | 39.50 | 39.80 | 38.85 | 39.70 |
| 7/10/75 | 39.75 | 41.12 | 39.75 | 40.90 |
| 7/11/75 | 41.00 | 41.20 | 40.50 | 41.10 |
| 7/14/75 | 41.25 | 41.80 | 41.05 | 41.80 |
| 7/15/75 | 41.80 | (41.97) | 40.30 | 40.90 |
| 7/16/75 | 41.45 | 41.45 | 40.25 | 40.60 |
| 7/17/75 | 40.35 | 40.50 | 39.30 | 39.80 |
| 7/18/75 | 39.55 | 40.45 | (39.20) | 40.15 |
| 7/21/75 | 40.50 | 41.25 | 40.40 | 41.03 |
| 7/22/75 | 41.20 | 41.65 | 41.00 | 41.60 |
| 7/23/75 | 41.60 | 41.67 | 41.22 | 41.32 |
| 7/24/75 | 41.60 | 41.95 | 41.55 | 41.57 |
| 7/25/75 | 41.70 | 42.60 | 41.55 | 42.45 |
| 7/28/75 | 42.50 | ((43.20)) | 42.40 | 42.77 |
| 7/29/75 | 42.07 | 42.15 | (41.10) | 41.87 |
| 7/30/75 | 42.75 | (42.75) | 41.70 | 42.42 |
| 7/31/75 | 41.30 | 41.35 | 40.10 | 40.10 |
| 8/01/75 | 40.40 | 40.40 | 39.35 | 39.60 |
| 8/04/75 | 39.20 | 39.70 | 38.80 | 39.00 |
| 8/05/75 | 38.75 | 39.30 | ((38.55)) | 39.30 |
| 8/06/75 | 39.22 | 39.80 | 38.95 | 39.42 |
| 8/07/75 | 39.60 | 40.80 | 39.60 | 40.75 |
| 8/08/75 | 40.50 | 40.85 | 40.00 | 40.32 |
| 8/11/75 | 40.50 | 41.20 | 40.50 | 41.05 |
| 8/12/75 | 40.70 | (41.65) | 40.30 | 40.55 |
| 8/13/75 | 40.70 | 41.20 | (40.30) | 41.00 |
| 8/14/75 | 41.05 | 41.25 | 40.70 | 40.97 |
| 8/15/75 | 40.82 | 41.47 | 40.75 | 41.40 |
| 8/18/75 | 41.05 | 41.47 | 40.95 | 41.17 |
| 8/19/75 | 41.07 | 42.00 | 41.05 | 41.97 |
| 8/20/75 | 42.37 | 42.80 | 42.25 | 42.77 |
| 8/21/75 | 42.75 | 43.75 | 42.65 | 43.70 |

Table 10. DEC CATTLE Price Data

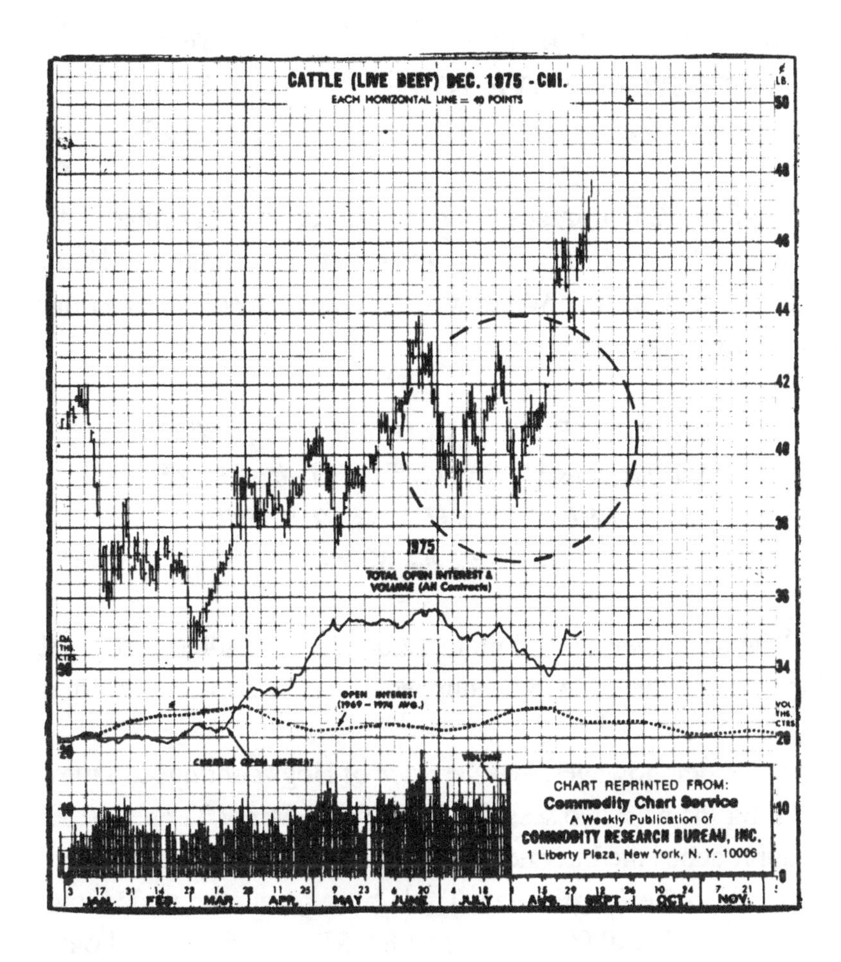
CATTLE (LIVE BEEF) DEC. 1975 - CHI.
EACH HORIZONTAL LINE = 40 POINTS
1975
TOTAL OPEN INTEREST & VOLUME (All Contracts)
OPEN INTEREST (1969 - 1974 AVG.)
VOLUME
CHART REPRINTED FROM:
Commodity Chart Service
A Weekly Publication of
COMMODITY RESEARCH BUREAU, INC.
1 Liberty Plaza, New York, N. Y. 10006
JAN. FEB. MAR. APR. MAY JUNE JULY AUG. SEPT. OCT. NOV.

| | |
|---|---|
| ***BUY STOP DEC HOG*** | ***49.70*** |
| ***PLACE PROTECTIVE STOP*** | ***48.57*** |
| ***OBJECTIVE*** | ***52.95*** |

Twenty-four (24) minutes later, the order was executed. By Tuesday, 8/19, the Critical Price was penetrated, and by 7:34 a.m., Wednesday, 8/20, the Window (51.77) was reached. Another broker order was given:

***CANCEL PROTECTIVE STOP 49.70***
***OFFSET TRADE UPON ANY PULL-BACK OF 79 POINTS, FROM THE HIGHEST PRICE REACHED, OR OFFSET AT 52.95.***

The price then moved up to 52.00 and pulled-back to 51.02, which caused the trade to be stopped out at 51.20 with a profit of $450.00.

Consider, however, that the price of Hogs continued to move up during the next two sessions through the Minor Target (52.95) and approached the Intermediate Target (IT) (54.13), by moving to 53.82. (Had the Intermediate Trade been taken, the trade would have yielded $1140.00. Entry at 48.82, SD = 1.16, stopped out at 52.65.) However, the idea to remember is: ***A TRADER NEVER GOES BROKE BY TAKING A PROFIT.***

## TRADE OFFSET AT TARGET

Trident Targets are realized in a majority of cases. The Window-Stop Differential Strategy will intercede frequently, however, preventing the full trade profit potential from being realized.

Full trade profit (Target reached) can be expected to occur approximately 40% of the time during profitable trades (60% of the time, the trade is stopped out by the SD). The trading odds can be improved, but only through careful analysis of the next higher swing level and the assumption of greater risk.

Certain Trident Trades carry a higher probability of reaching the Target than others. The first trade after a higher level peak or valley is statistically better than a trade whose Target is in the price region of the higher level Target. Through experience, a Trident Trader will learn to recognize and evaluate which trades are best and whether or not there is a high probability of reaching the Target.

Trident Trades which progress to the Target are perhaps one of the most fulfilling of all experiences in the market. Consider the following example.

### *Trade Analysis*

Inspection of Cattle price data (Table 10) through 7/16/75 reveals a significant fact. The ring low (38.25) on 7/8/75 is lower than the previous ring low (39.35, 7/3/75) and the ring high (41.97, 7/15/75) is higher than the previous ring high (40.77, 7/7/75). Clearly a trend change has occurred, that is, the trend of the market has changed from a falling market to a rising market. The ring low (38.25) is an Intermediate terminus. (The word terminus was first used in a Trident seminar by a student and friend from Canada during a brief discourse on the use and application of Fibonacci numbers.)

A Trident Trade to the upside can be expected to form sometime after a new P3 low is established below the current low (40.25, 7/16/75). Assume the next day's low (39.30) to be the new

| TRIDENT PRICES | | | TARGET PRICE | CRITICAL PRICE | ENTRY PRICE | PROFIT AMOUNT | STOP PROTECTED | STOP DIFFERENTIAL | RISK AMOUNT |
|---|---|---|---|---|---|---|---|---|---|
| $P_1$ | $P_2$ | $P_3$ | | | | | | | |
| 38.25 | 41.97 | 39.20 | 42.92 | 41.06 | 40.13 | $1,116. | 39.19 | -.69 | $277.00 |

Table 11. Minor Information Line — CATTLE TRADE

P3, then confirmation of this new P3 will occur if the market should rise 93 points to 40.23. However, this did not occur. In fact, the market had a closing range of 39.80 to 40.00; 23 points shy of triggering a new trade.

On 7/18 (the next day), a lower low was established (39.20) shortly after the opening. Consider the following example: P1 (38.25), P2 (41.97), and P3 (39.20) are well formed and represent the first clear tradeable minor swing in (Table 11) the new rising trend direction.

An order was given, 8:10 a.m., 7/18:

| | |
|---|---|
| ***BUY STOP CATTLE*** | ***40.15*** |
| ***PLACE PROTECTIVE STOP*** | ***39.17*** |
| ***OBJECTIVE*** | ***42.92*** |

By 9:45 a.m., the trade was executed and a new trade was in progress.

During the next trading session, on 7/21, the Critical Price (41.07) was reached and surpassed. The broker was instructed:

| | |
|---|---|
| ***CANCEL PROTECTIVE STOP*** | ***39.17*** |
| ***PLACE NEW PROTECTIVE STOP*** | ***40.15*** |

Four days later the Window (42.00) was penetrated and the following broker order was given:

***CANCEL PROTECTIVE STOP*** ***40.15***
***OFFSET TRADE UPON ANY PULL-BACK OF 69 POINTS, FROM THE HIGHEST PRICE REACHED, OR OFFSET AT 42.92.***

During the next trading session (7/28) and shortly after the market opened, the target was reached and exceeded (28 points) producing a gross profit of $1,108.00.

During the time that the Minor trade developed, an Intermediate level swing (38.25 to 43.20) had formed. By 7/31, it was apparent that an Intermediate reaction swing was in progress (this assumption is based upon the lower low 40.10 and the lower ringed high 42.75). Any rally below the current low (40.10) of 124 points,

$$\frac{(43.20 - 38.25)}{4}$$

would signal possible information of a new Intermediate low, $I_3$.

On 8/5, a new low was formed (38.55) shortly after the opening and held throughout that day. Consider the following Intermediate trade (Table 12):

***10:12 a.m. Wednesday 8/6*** the order was given:

| | |
|---|---|
| ***BUY STOP DEC CATTLE*** | ***39.80*** |
| ***PROTECTIVE STOP*** | ***38.52*** |
| ***OBJECTIVE*** | ***43.50*** |

The market was at 39.55 and moving up. The trade was executed shortly after the opening on 8/7.

***10:17 a.m. Monday 8/11.*** The Critical Price (41.02) had been reached and Protective Stops were moved to Entry 39.80 (Profit to Critical Price $488). By this time, the Intermediate price swing was well established and the trade was statistically risk free.

| TRIDENT PRICES | | | TARGET PRICE | CRITICAL PRICE | ENTRY PRICE | PROFIT AMOUNT | STOP PROTECTED | STOP DIFFERENTIAL | RISK AMOUNT |
|---|---|---|---|---|---|---|---|---|---|
| $I_1$ | $I_2$ | $I_3$ | | | | | | | |
| 38.25 | 43.20 | 38.55 | 43.50 | 41.02 | 39.80 | $1,480. | 38.52 | 1.16 | $496.00 |

Table 12. Trident Information Line — INTERMEDIATE CATTLE TRADE

***9:36 a.m. Tuesday 8/21.*** The Window was reached and by 10:20 a.m. the Target was reached. The trade occurred over twelve (12) trading sessions, but it took only three (3) sessions to reach the Critical Price. However, $1,480 for each contract traded was ample profit to reinforce the great pleasure from trading the Trident Strategy.

While the Intermediate trade developed, a significant Minor trade was expected to form based on $P_1 = I_3$ (38.55). By 8/12, $P_2$ formed (41.65) and $P_3$ was expected to form below the current low (40.30). However, by 8/13, it was apparent that the market would not move below (40.30) (Table 13). At 9:25 a.m. the following broker order was given:

| | |
|---|---|
| ***BUY STOP DEC CATTLE*** | ***41.07*** |
| ***PLACE PROTECTIVE STOP*** | ***40.27*** |
| ***OBJECTIVE*** | ***43.40*** |

By 8/19 (10:25 a.m.) both the Window and Critical Price were penetrated (note that the Window occurs before the Critical Price, which is not significantly uncommon in some Trident Trades). A new broker order was given:

***CANCEL PROTECTIVE STOP 40.27***
***OFFSET TRADE UPON ANY PULL-BACK 34 POINTS FROM THE HIGHEST PRICE REACHED OR OFFSET AT 43.40.***

Shortly before completion of the current Intermediate trade, the Minor Target was reached and exceeded, producing a profit of $930.

By taking advantage of two significant Minor trades along with the Intermediate trade which formed during the major swing (38.25 to 43.75) tremendous profit optimization occurred. Had a wise and prudent trader bought cattle at 38.25 (7/8) and sold the contract at 43.75 (8/21) that trader would have made $2,200.00. The three Trident Trades, however, had a combined profit of $3,518.00. Not only did the three Trident Trades realize $1,318.00 more than the basic move, but the Trident Trades were accomplished in 8 fewer trading sessions!

| TRIDENT PRICES | | | TARGET PRICE | CRITICAL PRICE | ENTRY PRICE | PROFIT AMOUNT | STOP PROTECTED | STOP DIFFERENTIAL | RISK AMOUNT |
|---|---|---|---|---|---|---|---|---|---|
| $P_1$ | $P_2$ | $P_3$ | | | | | | | |
| 38.55 | 41.65 | 40.30 | 43.40 | 41.85 | 41.07 | $930.00 | 40.27 | -.34 | $308.00 |

Table 13. Minor Information Line — CATTLE TRADE

# TRIDENT TRADE CRITERIA

# CHAPTER 5

The Commodity Market abounds with an ever changing panorama of price action and potential trade opportunities. So much so that the most diligent and prudent trader is constantly challenged to do his best each trading day. The tests and challenges are unrelenting but cry out and demand that the Trident Trader be skillful in his task lest he pay the awesome price of loss of capital and self condemnation. Thus is the way of the Commodity Market, unceasing in a perennial effort to separate the trader from his capital. But the Commodity Market exists as an objective reality, victimized and locked in by its own statistical rules. When understood, these rules render the market harmless, friendly and quite willing to surrender its profits to those who would desire to master it.

A strategy conceived in observable phenomenon is the master of any situation, no matter how perplexing, provided its user know, and adhere to the rules and procedures that govern that strategy. The Trident Trading Strategy is not different; there are rules and procedures which separate the wise user from the fool. Rules and procedures, which when followed, supplement and replace experience gained from trial and error.

The Trident Strategy hinges upon the single ability to recognize a tradeable situation. The theory, as applied, works; but the theory superficially applied could lead to chaos, loss of capital and frustration. Poor results are strictly a function of the degree of diligence and determination on the part of the Trident Trader.

(Trident Traders who do not develop early the habit of diligent application of all the rules have only themselves to blame.)

The single significant skill required to master the Trident Trading Strategy is the ability to expect, recognize and use the correct P3. Given the correct P3 for each and every trade, the positive results achieved far exceed 90% trade success. Trade success of this magnitude is well worth the effort to apply a few rules and statistical tests.

## FORMATION OF P3

The proper P3 exists as an illusionary mystery for many Trident Traders. Rules and tests for P3 have been developed to assist in predetermination of P3 validity. There are three (3) primary tests which greatly assist in determining whether or not the P3 selected is valid. Consistent application of each test will lead to profitable, low risk trading. The three (3) tests are as follows:

1. Peak or Valley Qualifications.
2. Price Region Qualification.
3. Action-Reaction Qualification.

These three (3) empirical tests, operating mutually together, constitute important objective criteria to ensure pleasurable, rewarding and relatively risk-free trading.

## PEAK AND VALLEY QUALIFICATION

Price swing analysis constitutes the fundamental thesis of the Trident Trading Strategy. Price swings are an integral part of market price action. Therefore, assumptions based upon price swing action have a high probability for validity. The current price of a given commodity can be described as a function of price up-swing or price down-swing. P3 represents a unique price because it's the last price of one swing and the first price of the next swing. For this reason there can be but ***one and only one P3*** which can establish and operate as a permanent beacon for positive trade decisions.

Given price data reflecting daily highs and lows, selection of P1 and P2 is a matter of working with statistical fact; however, P3 can only be determined as an assumptive presumption of fact. Nevertheless, P3 must be selected using the same basic principles applied to the selection of P1 and P2.

### *Analysis*

The price data (Table 14) reflects daily high/low statistics (Cocoa May 76). It is simple and straightforward to select P1 and P2. Starting in the column for daily lows, it is clear that P1 (68.35, 3/30) is lower than the previous day's low (68.90, 2/2) and lower than the following day's low (69.40, 3/31). Likewise, it is clear that P2 (71.15, 4/1) is higher than the previous day's high (70.61, 3/31) and higher than the following day's high (70.90, 4/2). But suppose the market had just opened on 4/2 (70.82)? What objective criteria can be used to determine whether or not a valid P3 was established? Should the previous day's low (70.35) be assumed a valid P3? Should a broker order be given based upon P1 (68.35), P2 (71.15), P3 (70.35) or should the order wait for some other signal? Consider the following rule-definition (Minor Swings):

***A peak is a price that is higher than the previous day's high, and higher than the following day's high; likewise, a valley***

Commodity: *COCOA MAY 1976*

| DATE | OPEN | HIGH | LOW | CLOSE |
|---|---|---|---|---|
| 2/29/76 | 70.40 | (70.45) | 68.90 | 69.20 |
| 3/30/76 | 68.45 | 69.80 | (68.35) | 69.75 |
| 3/31/76 | 69.45 | 70.61 | 69.40 | 70.10 |
| 4/01/76 | 70.80 | (71.15) | 70.35 | 70.50 |
| 4/02/76 | 70.82 | 70.90 | (69.75) | 70.15 |
| 4/05/76 | 70.40 | 72.15 | 69.95 | 71.95 |
| 4/06/76 | 73.18 | 73.90 | 72.90 | 73.90 |

Table 14. COCOA Price Data

***is a price that is lower than the previous day's low, and lower than the following day's low.*** (A similar rule-definition holds true for Intermediate, Major and Micro Swings.)

This rule-definition is called the ***Peak-Valley Qualification Test*** (referred to as ringing). In the example above (Table 14), the question of whether or not the low (70.35, 4/1) should be acted upon can be examined using the Peak-Valley Qualification Test. The first element of the test is: ***a price that is lower than the previous day's low.*** The previous day's low was lower than the suspected P3 (69.40, 3/3). Consequently, 70.35 fails the first criterion of the test. It follows, then, that the P3 desired would have to be less than (or equal to) 70.35; an event that has not yet occurred.

Using the same price data (Table 14) what can be said of the market (4/2) near the close? Should a broker order be given? At sometime prior to the close a new low was established (69.75, 4/2). Will this new low (69.75) meet the Peak-Valley Qualification Test?

***Lower than the previous day's low*** — 69.75 is certainly lower than 70.35.

***Lower than the following day's low*** — Unknown until the close of the following day's market. Therefore, assume P3 confirmation if entry price (70.45) is reached.

The Peak-Valley Qualification Test must be reasoned in this precise manner, because ***P3 is assumptive*** and proven valid only as a result of a future event. (It is significant that entry was reached (4/5) and the target objective realized with an added bonus of 63 points due to the "GAP UP" opening (4/6); trade profit, $819.00.)

The Peak-Valley Qualification Test applies to Major, Intermediate and Micro swings. Each level has an objective and assumptive condition, which when applied will screen out superficial M3s, I3s, and F3s (fluctuations of Micro swings). The general form of the Peak-Valley Rule-Definition is as follows:

> ***A (swing-level) peak is a price that is higher than the previous (subordinate swing-level) high, and higher than the following (subordinate swing-level) high; likewise, a (swing-level) valley is a price that is lower than the previous (subordinate swing-level) low and lower than the following (subordinate swing-level) low.*** (Where swing-level means Major, Intermediate, Minor or Micro and subordinate swing-level means next lower swing level, e.g. Intermediate, Minor, tick, etc.).

## PHANTOM PEAKS AND VALLEYS

The Peak-Valley Qualification Test cannot be applied in certain cases. Occasionally two or more consecutive peaks occur without a clear valley formation. Likewise, several consecutive valleys will form without an intervening peak. The missing peak or valley does exit. But only through careful analysis of price data can the missing peak or valley be found. Poorly formed peaks and valleys are called ***Phantoms***.

The Phantom Peak (Table 15) results from the two consecutive valleys (13.75, 1/13; 14.90, 1/19). It is logical to assume that there is one, and only one, highest price (peak) between the two lows (valleys). Observe the high (15.50, 1/16) followed by a substantially lower market opening price the following session (15.08, 1/19). Clearly, 15.50 was the highest price reached prior to the subsequent low (14.90, 1/19). Therefore, the one and only highest price reached (peak) between the two lows (valleys) was the ***Phantom Peak,*** 15.50.

The Phantom Valley (Table 16) results from formation of two consecutive peaks (3.99, 11/5; 3.83, 11/11). There can be one, and only one, lowest price (valley) between two consecutive peaks. The price low (3.75, 11/10), was the lowest price reached after the first peak (3.99, 11/5). Observe the higher opening (3.80, 11/11) versus the lower closing price (3.68 ½) on the same day. The ring high (3.83) formed prior to the lower close (3.68 ½). Consequently, the low price (3.75) was the lowest price reached (valley) prior to the high (3.83). Therefore, the one and only low price between the two peaks was the ***Phantom Valley,*** 3.75.

## PRICE REGIONS AND QUALIFICATION TESTS

Once the trader has qualified the potential P3 through application of the Peak-Valley Rule, the next test is whether or not the potential P3 has formed in a reasonable price region. Since each price swing has an ideal target, it is axiomatic that P3 should form in the vicinity of that target. However, a valid P3 may form before or after the ideal target. For this reason, it is necessary to develop a ***Window*** concept which will set up a region of "P3 expectancy," consistent with valid Trident assumptions.

Commodity price action produces both action and reaction swings. P3's that form the basis for new trades occur as the last price level of a reaction swing and the first price level of a new action swing. Each Commodity Market can be expected to react in a similar manner as the last previous reaction (the future is based upon the immediate past).

Commodity: *POTATOES MAY 1976*

| DATE | OPEN | HIGH | LOW | CLOSE |
|---|---|---|---|---|
| 1/09/76 | 14.25 | 14.25 | 13.80 | 14.12 |
| 1/12/76 | 14.62 | (14.62) | 14.25 | 14.25 |
| 1/13/76 | 14.05 | 14.10 | (13.75) | 13.75 |
| 1/14/76 | 14.25 | 14.25 | 14.25 | 14.25 |
| 1/15/76 | 14.75 | 14.75 | 14.75 | 14.75 |
| 1/16/76 | 15.50 | (15.50)Ph. | 15.30 | 15.50 |
| 1/19/76 | 15.08 | 16.00 | (14.90) | 15.75 |
| 1/20/76 | 16.25 | 16.25 | 16.00 | 16.25 |

Table 15. Phantom Peak

Commodity: *WHEAT MAR 1975*

| DATE | OPEN | HIGH | LOW | CLOSE |
|---|---|---|---|---|
| 11/03/75 | 3.980 | 3.980 | 3.884 | 3.892 |
| 11/04/75 | 3.892 | 3.954 | (3.874) | 3.936 |
| 11/05/75 | 3.920 | (3.990) | 3.920 | 3.946 |
| 11/06/75 | 3.944 | 3.946 | 3.844 | 3.872 |
| 11/07/75 | 3.880 | 3.900 | 3.840 | 3.846 |
| 11/10/75 | 3.810 | 3.820 | (3.750)Ph. | 3.780 |
| 11/11/75 | 3.800 | (3.830) | 3.680 | 3.685 |
| 11/12/75 | 3.690 | 3.690 | 3.565 | 3.635 |

Table 16. Phantom Valley

Each reaction swing has a discrete minimum resemblance (determinate) to the previous reaction swing (this idea can be related to the concept of Critical Price relative to action swings).

The minimum significant resemblance, or reaction ***determinate,*** can be thought of as a price level ***beyond*** $(P_3 + T)/2$ or simply, a price region beyond one half of the last reaction swing. This price, called a ***determinate,*** is defined as follows:

***DETERMINATE*** $= .625\,(P_2 - P_1) + P_3$

***WHERE*** $P_3$ ***IS THE LAST PRICE LEVEL OF THE CURRENT ACTION SWING.***

The ***determinate*** is, therefore, merely the minimum last price level for a new reaction swing.

Formation of a higher level swing (Intermediate, Major) results in a change of trend direction for dependent subordinate action swings. Each time a higher level swing terminates, two consecutive subordinate action swings will form, i.e. the last action swing in the previous trend direction followed by the first action swing in a new trend direction. It is not uncommon, therefore, to mistake a valid action swing for a reaction swing, or vice versa. The rule to remember is: ***if*** $P_2 = I_3$ ***then the two swings*** $P_1 - P_2$ ***and*** $P_2 - P_3$ ***are valid subordinate action swings in opposite directions*** (Subordinate Action Swing Rule).

Calculating a particular ***determinate***, after application of the Subordinate Action Swing Rule, involves analysis of sufficient price data to determine the comparable last reaction swing. The reaction ***determinate*** after application of the Subordinate Action Swing Rule is defined as follows:

***DETERMINATE = .625 ($P_0$ - $P_1$) + $P_3$***

***WHERE $P_0$ IS THE PEAK OR VALLEY JUST PRIOR TO $P_1$.***

## TREND REVERSAL

During the formation of $P_3$, the reaction target (T) can be exceeded. If (T) is exceeded by a substantial amount, then what was considered to be a reaction swing may, in fact, be an action swing (first action swing in a new direction). The degree to which a reaction target is exceeded has the same effect as applying brakes to a moving automobile; the greater the overshot, the greater the trend retardation. The precise price at which ***Trend Reversal*** (retardation) occurs cannot be accurately determined. However, retracement beyond the previous Critical Price $(P_2 + P_3)/2$, would be assumptive evidence that trading interest in that trend direction has started to wane.

Trend retardation (taking the steam out of a market) occurs frequently and results often in sluggish (flat) price action. Trades predicated on slow moving markets produce varied results and, although trade profits are available, such profits are slow to develop. For this reason an objective rule must be applied which would tend to signal price trend retardation possibilities. Consider the following definition:

***TREND REVERSAL PRICE = .625 ($P_2$ - $P_3$) + $P_3$***

If $P_3$ forms beyond the Trend Reversal Price, then the trade will not yield its full potential (the exception to this rule is if $P_1 = I_3$).

## P3 WINDOW

The P3 Window is a price region which starts at the ***Reaction Determinate*** and extends to the ***Trend Reversal Price.*** A new P3 formed within the P3 Window will lead to profitable trades. (Rapidly accelerating markets sometimes exhibit reaction swings which are abrupt and may not enter the Reaction Window on at least the first reaction after a major breakout swing.)

Based upon the price data in Table 14, the P3 Window would be calculated as follows:

P1 (70.45), P2 (68.35), P3 (71.15)

$$
\begin{aligned}
\text{DETERMINATE PRICE} &= .625\,(P2 - P1) + P3 \\
&= .625\,(68.35 - 70.45) + 71.15 \\
&= .625\,(-2.1) + 71.15 \\
&= -1.31 + 71.15 \\
&= \underline{69.83}
\end{aligned}
$$

$$
\begin{aligned}
\text{TREND REVERSAL PRICE} &= .625\,(P2 - P3) + P3 \\
&= .625\,(68.35 - 70.15) + 71.15 \\
&= .625\,(-2.8) + 71.15 \\
&= -1.75 + 71.15 \\
&= \underline{69.40}
\end{aligned}
$$

The new P3 can be expected to form within the price region lower than (or equal to) 69.83 (Determinate Price) and higher than (or equal to) 69.40 (Trend Reversal Price). In other words, once the reaction swing begins, the possibility of a new P3 need not be considered until the price has entered the P3 Window.

The concept of a reaction target is not significant, because little predictive evidence is gained by the casual fact that a reaction target was reached. In the example above, the reaction target was 69.05, which is substantially beyond the P3 Window. Had the reaction swing extended to the reaction target, then the trend reversal limit would have been exceeded and the current up-trend retarded. In addition, the subsequent trade to the upside would have to be avoided in favor of a possible trade to the downside.

(It is significant that a new qualified P3 formed at 69.75, eight (8) points within the P3 Window. A Trident Trade based upon that P3 can be expected to perform rapidly and well; and ***so it did.***)

## P3 WINDOW ANALYSIS

The P3 Window is formed by the price region bounded by two (2) significant indicators. The ***Reaction Determinate Price*** (DP) represents the start of the P3 Window (except in certain instances when the current P2 = I3). The ***Trend Reversal Price*** (TRP) represents the end of the P3 Window (same exception applies). The ***Determinate Price*** is used to prevent a premature search for P3 . The ***Trend Reversal Price*** is used to signal a probable trend reversal, which prevents a poor trade from being entered. Proper analysis of price action using the P3 Window indicators greatly reduces the risk of poor trade selection. Likewise, the P3 Window provides an excellent tool for preparing traders in advance of market action.

The following trade sequence will illustrate the use of P3 Window Analysis Techniques; consider the first Trident (Table 17):

P1 ($4.47^{0}$), P2 ($4.64^{5}$), P3 ($4.39^{0}$)

The swing P2 ($4.64^5$) to P3 ($4.39^0$) reveals action on the downside. The next swing should be a reaction forming a new P3 for the next trade to the downside. A new P3 should form within the P3 Window:

DETERMINATE PRICE = .625 (P2 - P1) + P3
= .625 ($4.64^5$ - $4.47^0$) + $4.39^0$
= .625 (1.75) + $4.39^0$
= .109 + $4.39^0$
= <u>4.499</u>

TREND REVERSAL PRICE = .625 (P2 - P3) + P3
= .625 ($4.64^5$ - $4.39^0$) + $4.39^0$
= .625 (.255) + $4.39^0$
= .159 + $4.39^0$
= <u>4.549</u>

However, the close of the market on 9/9 was $4.60^0$, well above and beyond the P3 Window, indicating a trend reversal or retardation. The opening price ($4.77^7$) the next day confirmed a trend change by establishing a higher high (previous high $4.64^5$, 9/4). The action had now changed to the upside; a downside reaction should occur providing an opportunity to buy the next action (upside). Consider the next Trident:

P1 ($4.64^5$), P2 ($4.39^0$), P3 ($4.70^0$)

A ***Trend Reversal*** was confirmed during the last action swing ($4.39^0$ to $4.70^0$). P2 ($4.39^0$) represents an Intermediate valley (I3), because $4.39^0$ was the lowest Minor low prior to establishment of

**Commodity:** ***SILVER DEC 1975***

| DATE | OPEN | HIGH | LOW | CLOSE |
|---|---|---|---|---|
| 8/29/75 | 4.757 | 4.765 | 4.635 | 4.670 |
| 9/02/75 | 4.480 | 4.515 | (4.470) | 4.470 |
| 9/03/75 | 4.550 | 4.600 | 4.528 | 4.592 |
| 9/04/75 | 4.640 | (4.645) | 4.535 | 4.610 |
| 9/05/75 | 4.593 | 4.615 | 4.560 | 4.610 |
| 9/08/75 | 4.585 | 4.585 | 4.530 | 4.530 |
| 9/09/75 | 4.540 | 4.670 | ((4.390)) | 4.600 |
| 9/10/75 | 4.667 | (4.700) | 4.615 | 4.660 |
| 9/11/75 | 4.620 | 4.650 | (4.585) | 4.615 |
| 9/12/75 | 4.650 | ((4.750)) | 4.650 | 4.723 |
| 9/15/75 | 4.700 | 4.720 | 4.685 | 4.700 |
| 9/16/75 | 4.663 | (4.725) | (4.640) | 4.645 |
| 9/17/75 | 4.595 | 4.700 | (4.545)Ph. | 4.692 |
| 9/18/75 | 4.655 | (4.700) | 4.535 | 4.577 |
| 9/19/75 | 4.675 | 4.675 | 4.500 | 4.533 |
| 9/20/75 | 4.530 | 4.580 | ((4.445)) | 4.495 |
| 9/23/75 | 4.460 | 4.555 | 4.460 | 4.492 |
| 9/24/75 | 4.555 | 4.600 | 4.525 | 4.583 |
| 9/25/75 | 4.575 | 4.610 | 4.545 | 4.552 |
| 9/26/75 | 4.560 | (4.625) | 4.560 | 4.570 |
| 9/27/75 | 4.585 | 4.625 | (4.505) | 4.510 |
| 9/30/75 | 4.557 | 4.585 | 4.520 | 4.537 |
| 10/01/75 | 4.587 | ((4.645)) | 4.550 | 4.602 |
| 10/02/75 | 4.635 | 4.645 | 4.515 | 4.545 |
| 10/03/75 | 4.525 | 4.525 | (4.415) | 4.470 |
| 10/06/75 | 4.497 | 4.505 | 4.440 | 4.480 |

Table 17. SILVER DEC 1975

a higher Minor high. The ***Subordinate Swing Rule*** must be applied, since the swing $P_1$ ($4.64^5$) to $P_2$ ($4.39^0$) is a subordinate action swing and $P_2$ ($4.39^0$) to $P_3$ ($4.70^0$) is a subordinate action swing as well. The last subordinate reaction swing was, therefore, $P_0$ ($4.47^0$) to $P_1$ ($4.64^5$). A new $P_3$ should form within the Window:

$$
\begin{aligned}
\text{DETERMINATE PRICE} &= .625\,(P_0 - P_1) + P_3 \\
&= .625\,(4.47^0 - 4.64^5) + 4.70^0 \\
&= .625\,(-.175) + 4.70^0 \\
&= \underline{4.59}^0
\end{aligned}
$$

$$
\begin{aligned}
\text{TREND REVERSAL PRICE} &= .625\,(P_2 - P_3) + P_3 \\
&= .625\,(4.39^0 - 4.70^0) + 4.70^0 \\
&= .625\,(-.31) + 4.70^0 \\
&= \underline{4.50}^6
\end{aligned}
$$

A tradeable $P_3$ formed just inside the $P_3$ Window ($4.58^5$). The Information Line for the trade is as follows (see Table 18). Shortly after the market opened (9/12) the trade entry ($4.66^2$) was reached. The Window ($4.70^1$) was penetrated during that same session and the Stop Differential applied. Toward the end of the trading day, the high ($4.75^0$) was reached and the trade stopped out with a profit ($4.72^1$), $295. (It is significant that the Critical Price ($4.74^0$) was barely exceeded, because the market did fail to hold the up trend at that price ($4.75^0$).

The next Trident:

$P_1$ ($4.70^0$), $P_2$ ($4.58^5$), $P_3$ ($4.75^0$)

indicates action on the upside, looking for a reaction into the $P_3$ Window for the next trade up. A new $P_3$ should form within:

DETERMINATE PRICE $= .625\,(P_2 - P_1) + P_3$
$= .625\,(4.58^5 - 4.70^0) + 4.75^0$
$= \underline{4.67^8}$

TREND REVERSAL PRICE $= .625\,(P_2 - P_3) + P_3$
$= .625\,(4.58^5 - 4.70^0) + 4.75^0$
$= \underline{4.64^7}$

However, the reaction extended beyond the $P_3$ Window ($4.64^0$). Although close, this implies that the trend to the upside is now retarded or ready for reversal. This signals the possibility of a trade to the downside and, therefore, the current trade to the upside should be avoided. Accordingly, a $P_3$ Window can be constructed should the previous high ($4.75^0$) not be exceeded.

The next Trident:

$P_1$ ($4.58^5$), $P_2$ ($4.75^0$), $P_3$ ($4.64^0$)

The appearance of this Trident does not suggest a potential losing trade. The target ($4.80^5$) represents an interesting profit. But $P_3$ did form beyond the limits of the $P_3$ Window. Therefore, the analysis must shift to $P_2$ ($4.75^0$) as representing an Intermediate terminus ($I_3$). If $P_2$ ($4.75^0$) = $I_3$, then both swings $P_1$ - $P_2$ and $P_2$ - $P_3$ are subordinate action swings and the Subordinate Action Rule would have to be applied. Based upon the assumption that $P_2 = I_3$ , the next trade would be to the downside (this assumption would hold true so long as the price does not exceed $I_3$ ($4.75^0$). If, and only if, $P_2 = I_3$ a new $P_3$ should form within the $P_3$ Window:

| TRIDENT PRICES | | | TARGET PRICE | CRITICAL PRICE | ENTRY PRICE | PROFIT AMOUNT | STOP PROTECTED | STOP DIFFERENTIAL | RISK AMOUNT |
|---|---|---|---|---|---|---|---|---|---|
| $P_1$ | $P_2$ | $P_3$ | | | | | | | |
| $4.39^{0}$ | $4.70^{0}$ | $4.58^{5}$ | $4.89^{5}$ | $4.74^{0}$ | $4.66^{2}$ | $\$1162^{50}$ | $4.58^{4}$ | .029 | $385.00 |

Table 18. Trident Information Line — SILVER TRADE

DETERMINATE PRICE = $.625\ (P_0 - P_1) + P_3$
= $.625\ (4.70^{0} - 4.58^{5}) + 4.64^{0}$
= $.625\ (.115) + 4.64^{0}$
= $\underline{4.71}^{1}$

TREND REVERSAL PRICE = $.625\ (P_2 - P_3) + P_3$
= $.625\ (4.75^{0} - 4.64^{0}) + 4.64^{0}$
= $.625\ (.11) + 4.64^{0}$
= $\underline{4.70}^{8}$

Note that the Determinate Price, $4.71^{1}$, is greater than the Trend Reversal Price, $4.70^{8}$. The $P_3$ Window is ***inverted***, which means that the $P_3$ Window has a starting price ($4.71^{1}$) but does not terminate at a defined limit. But then the $P_3$ Window, in this instance, is based upon the assumption that the up trend is completed. The assumption holds true so long as the market does not move above $4.50^{0}$. Therefore, $4.75^{0}$ becomes the upper limit for purposes of assuming (confirmation) a trend reversal (from assuming down trend to confirming continuation of up trend). If $4.75^{0}$ holds as an Intermediate terminus $I_3$ during the next swing, then $4.75^{0}$ will be $P_1$ for the next trade and the ***Trend Reversal Price*** loses significance because the ***Two Swing Rule*** requires at least two subordinate action swings between Intermediate terminals. In other words, there would have to be at least one more action swing to the downside before another trend reversal could occur.

A tradeable $P_3$ formed within the $P_3$ Window ($4.72^{5}$), confirming the assumption that $4.75^{0}$ was an Intermediate terminus; the Information Line for the new trade (Table 19) is as follows: by the close of the market (9/16), the market has moved through the Critical Price ($4.67^{0}$) and settled at $4.64^{5}$. The open on 9/17, exceeded the trade objective and, therefore, the trade was offset at that price ($4.59^5$), producing a trade profit of $510.

The P3 Window, as an analytical tool, provides a significant opportunity for planning, avoiding unnecessary risk and increased market awareness. Analysis of the first Trident revealed and confirmed a trend reversal, which allowed planning for the first trade which made $295. The subsequent P3 Window Analysis called attention to another possible trend reversal, allowing a potentially losing trade to be avoided. Upon confirmation of a subsequent trend reversal, a second trade was entered, which yielded $510. It is significant that all these events transpired over a period of seven (7) trading sessions during a relatively flat price action market. The use and application of the P3 Window will keep the Trident Trader well in tune with positive market events and at the same time eliminate costly surprises.

## ACTION-REACTION QUALIFICATIONS

A reaction swing functions much like the accelerator and brake on an automobile. The smaller the reaction, the greater is the acceleration in the trend direction; the greater the trend is accelerated (action swing), the larger the reaction that can be expected. This kind of price action can be observed time and time again. Reaction swings are not very reliable, and for that reason, reaction targets must give way to price regions (P3 Window) in order to distinguish good tradeable possibilities.

***Reaction swings should not be traded*** because the trader has no positive control (strategy) over Protective Stops such as defined on action swings. There is no Window based upon rising-falling market trends, but only a calculated Window which may or may not

| TRIDENT PRICES | | | TARGET PRICE | CRITICAL PRICE | ENTRY PRICE | PROFIT AMOUNT | STOP PROTECTED | STOP DIFFERENTIAL | RISK AMOUNT |
|---|---|---|---|---|---|---|---|---|---|
| $P_1$ | $P_2$ | $P_3$ | | | | | | | |
| 4.75 | 4.64 | $4.72^5$ | $4.61^5$ | 4.67 | $4.69^7$ | $410.00 | $4.72^6$ | 2.12 | $140.00 |

Table 19. Trident Information Line — SILVER TRADE

apply. Only extreme greed, or ego, requires trading reaction swings (some Trident Traders have been known to attempt trading reaction swings, believing that P2 is a higher level price and a new trend change has occurred). The following rules should be observed:

***IF BUYING, THEN $P_3$ MUST BE GREATER THAN $P_1$.***

***IF SELLING, THEN $P_3$ MUST BE LESS THAN $P_1$.***

Observance of these two (2) rules will insure that only action swings are being traded.

## INTER-LEVEL CONFLICTS

Price action in the Commodity Market presents incredible mysteries to the uninformed trader. Perhaps the most startling mystery is the fact that price action (swings) occurs at various levels simultaneously. Minor, Intermediate, and Major price swings follow the same action-reaction rules, have ideal targets and form peaks and valleys. For this reason, three traders can trade the same market, entering at a technically correct Entry Price, manage Protective Stop application, and make a profit, yet each trader's experience could be different.

Commodity price action exhibits observable price phenomena, which although inexplicable, could be forecast with a degree of accuracy. The Intermediate price swing, for example, will contain at least two Minor action swings; a Major swing will contain at least two Intermediate action swings. This two swing minimum relationship between levels is a powerful key to forecasting and planning future trades.

There are rules, however, that effect the relationship between price swing levels which must be applied by the Trident Trader. The target of the next higher level price swing has priority over the target of the subordinate price swing. Inter-level target conflicts occur in two (2) instances:

1. The target objective of the subordinate swing is in opposition to the target objective of the next higher price swing.
2. The target objective of the subordinate price swing exceeds the target objective of the higher level price swing.

## TARGET OPPOSITION

Inter-level target conflict, in which a subordinate level objective exceeds the objective of the higher level price swing, must be resolved in favor of the higher level price swing. The higher level price swing will terminate upon the peak-valley formed by the last action swing of the subordinate level. For this reason, the last subordinate action swing in the vicinity of the higher level target will be followed by a subordinate level action swing in a new direction, and, therefore, increase the risk of loss (Figure 30). The following axiom applies:

***The target of a higher level swing is the assumed terminus for the current subordinate level action swing unless the subordinate action swing target does not exceed the higher level target.***

Perhaps the most common mistake made by Trident Traders is failure to examine the status of the next higher level swing. Each Trident Trade is based upon an action swing (assumed), which is

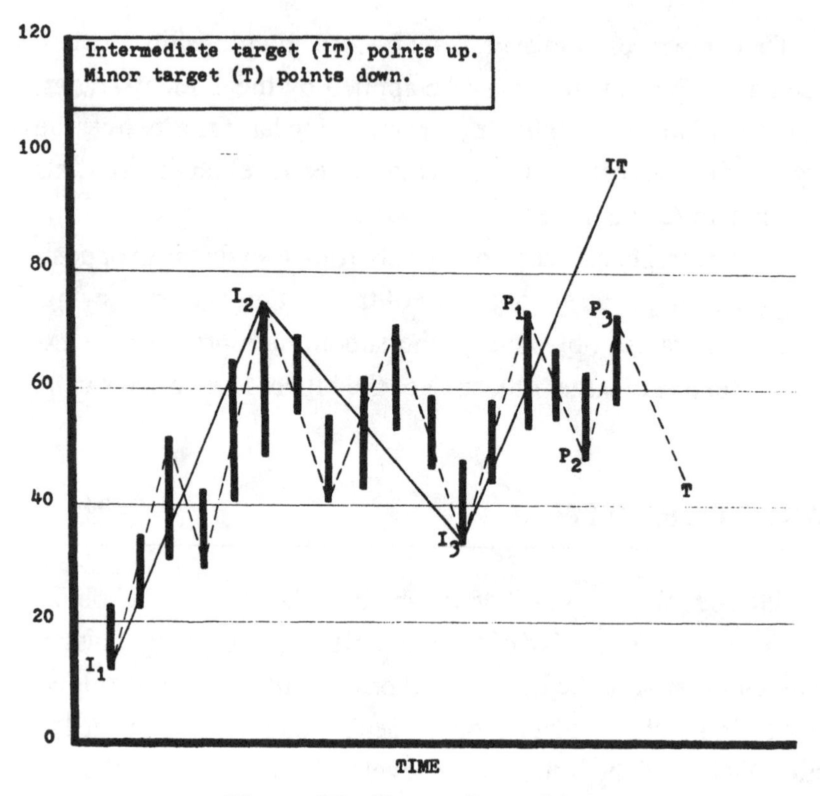


Figure 29. Target Opposition

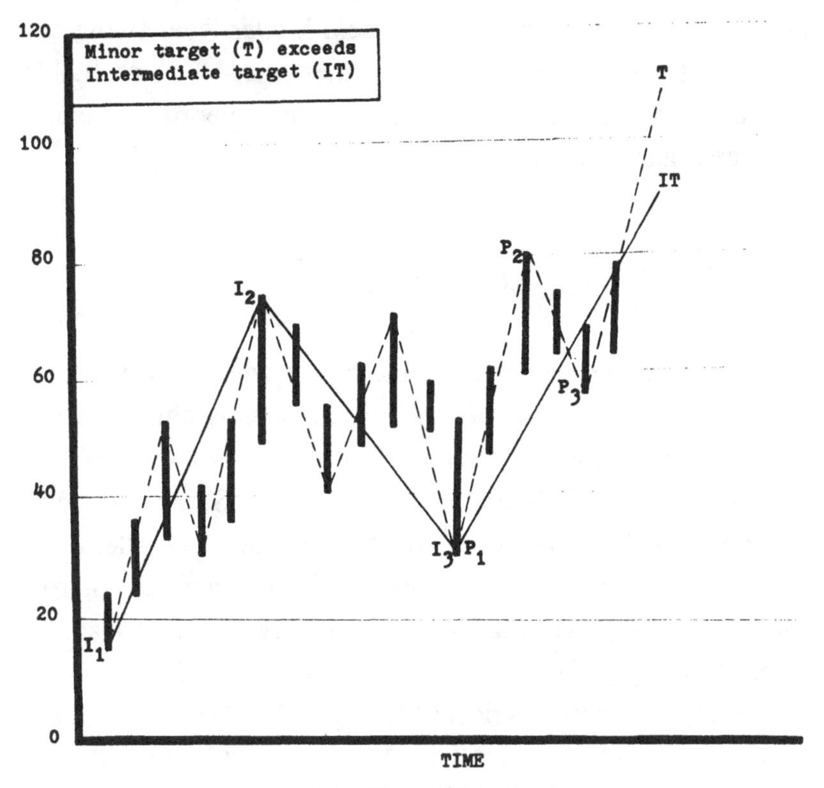


Figure 30. Target Limitation

dependent upon whether or not the next higher level swing has completed its move. In other words, there can be no profitable opportunity in the current trade unless that opportunity exists within the higher level swing currently in progress.

## TRADE SELECTION SUMMARY

The market, not the trader, determines what trade to make. ***Market price action is the only reality;*** the trader is simply there to capitalize on that reality. A trading strategy is a tool to enable the trader to act or not act at the proper time. Trident Strategy is a well developed tool that, when used properly, will serve a trader faithfully. Trident Strategy used improperly will separate the fool from his money quickly. The only skill required by a Trident Trader is the ability to ***apply the strategy correctly and completely.***

The key to successful Trident Trading is ***objectivity.*** One Trident Trade is no different from another, only the results may differ. The steps of research, analysis, and trade management are always the same. The data collected, broker orders, P3 qualification tests, the Trident Information Line, and the calculation of the higher level swing status, are the same for every Trident Trade. The trade that has just reached entry is not unique, nor will it become the world's greatest trade; that trade is nothing more than the trade made the previous day. Objectivity makes discipline an easy habit to master. Trident Strategy leaves little room for ego fantasies. The single objective is to make money! The sooner the trader becomes aware that trading commodities is to make money, the sooner the trader can realize that objective!

Trident Strategy was created for the purpose of trading commodities successfully. A Trident Trade resulting from proper application of Trident rules and procedures is an opportunity to make money. How much money is made becomes a simple function of how many Trident Trades can be made. The more trades made properly, the more money the trader can expect to make. Each commodity becomes an opportunity. Given a well qualified P3, nine trades in every ten (90%) can be expected to make a profit. Given a well qualified P3, high risk trades are automatically excluded.

There are no good or bad Trident Trades. There are only Trident Trades which make money or not. If the strategy requires a trade be made, then the trade should be made. The strategy has built-in odds which favor profit (3 to 1). Not taking a trade that is indicated because the trader believed the trade was bad, will not work. Taking a trade because the strategy indicated the trade is the only way to use Trident effectively. Therefore, the market, not the trader, determines when and at what price to buy, sell and take profit. ***The market is never wrong!***

# TRIDENT MARKET ANALYSIS

# CHAPTER 6

If a commodity trader knew in advance when the trend direction of the market would change, then commodity trading could literally be as simple as "Buying the low and Selling the high." But then, it should be the goal of any trading strategy to achieve that kind of trading simplicity. Many trend analysis systems devote much rigor to portend an ability to forecast trend changes. Some commodity traders, who are admittedly price action theorists, believe that their personal system of analysis can and will signal market trend changes. Books, seminars, newsletters and articles in magazines purport an ability to adequately forecast trend changes. Within all such claims of trend change predictability there is one fact that remains true, and that fact is:

***PRICE TRENDS CHANGE, AND A UNIQUE SIGNAL EXISTS WHICH TRIGGERS THAT CHANGE.***

Understanding the proper signal requires some fundamental understanding of what the market is attempting to do at a given time. The rewards of knowing market price action to the extent of trend changes are incalculable!

The Trident Strategy as previously discussed is complete from the standpoint of profitable, low risk trading. However, no matter how complete the mechanical strategy, understanding why something works is the ultimate mastery. Great tasting food, for example, is its own reward for many people, but understanding why the food tastes good and its nutritional benefits is an even greater reward for some people. There can be no enduring security or satisfaction in making large amounts of money without understanding the vehicle which makes the money possible. The Commodity Market is the vehicle, Trident Strategy is the key and understanding why the two go together is the ultimate opportunity.

Adequate planning is a prerequisite for any successful endeavor. To drive an automobile from Los Angeles to New York requires a road map and a plan. To attempt such a trip without a plan is to invite surprise and possible disaster. Trident market analysis is like a road map. Trident Trading Strategy is like a trip plan connecting sequential legs of a long journey.

Trident market analysis involves a detailed discussion of the consequences of the market seeking a stable balance between buyers and sellers. Imagine attempting to balance a broom in the palm of your hand and the individual motion of your hand while maintaining balance. Price action in the market exists in order to seek price balance and at the same time compensate for over balance. Yet, this chapter deals with analysis of the market within the consequences of Trident assumptions. The most basic and fundamental Trident assumption is that one and only one ideal target exists for each swing at each swing level and that ideal target is expressed as:

$$T = P_2 + P_3 - P_1$$

The key question that must be answered is: What is the consequence of not reaching (or exceeding) the target? It's the answer to this question which gives rise to the following ideas and concepts:

1. Variance.
2. Swing balance.
3. Trend changes.

Each concept is an integral part of Trident market analysis and the powerful techniques involved in literally buying the low and selling the high.

## VARIANCE

An ideal target exists for each swing at each swing level. But what is an ideal target? What is the significance if such a target is missed? The answer to this question and other similar questions is the subject of Target Variance and Variance analysis. It is true that ideal targets are seldom reached exactly. However, certain ideas concerning the net condition of a particular market can be known through analysis of the current peak (or valley) vs the target for the peak (or valley).

Consider a current peak or valley P3. Prior to formation of the current P3 there was a calculated target (T3). Compare the difference between P3 and T3 or:

$$(P3 - T3)$$

there are three (3) conditions which satisfy this relationship

$$P3 - T3 > 0.$$
$$P3 - T3 < 0.$$
$$P3 - T3 = 0.$$

If P3 - T3 is greater than zero, then the market can be thought of as gaining upward momentum, and the variance between P3 and T3 is positive. If P3 - T3 is less than zero than the market is losing momentum and the variance between P3 and T3 is negative. If P3 is equal to T3, then the market can be thought of as being in balance relative to the swing P2 to P3 .

Consider the swing P3 to P4. If during the previous swing the market gained momentum (P3 - T3 > 0) then that variance (P3 - T3) will be automatically incorporated into the new target T4 by the same amount. Likewise, if the difference between P3 and T3 were negative (lost momentum) then the target T4 would be lower by the amount of the difference (P3 - T3). If P3 - T3 were equal to zero, then T4 would reflect neither a gain or a loss of momentum.

Imagine the market in which each swing reflected a gain in momentum, i.e. each successive P3 - T3 > 0. If the original trend were in a downward direction, then eventually the downward trend would have to give way to an upward trend. In other words, each action swing to the downside would become shorter while each reaction swing to the upside would become longer, until eventually the reaction swings to the upside would exceed the action swings to the downside. Therefore, the ultimate net effect of P3 - T3 > 0 is to change the trend direction of the market upward. A similar argument can be given for the case where P3 - T3 < 0 or negative momentum. The net effect of continued negative momentum is to turn the trend of the market downward. Finally, if each target were reached exactly (P3 - T3 = 0) then the market would continue in the same trend direction without variation. (Just think, analysis of the variance between the last swing and its target is an important clue to what the market may be attempting to do upon the very next swing.)

## SWING BALANCE

Nature provides a vivid account of ongoing balances between opposing forces. The animal kingdom, for example, maintains a natural ecological balance between animal population and food supply. The economy exhibits a balance between supply and demand. Perhaps the most extraordinary balance is expressed in the rule that power only yields to power. In other words, applied power without opposition creates unceasing momentum.

The concept of swing balances is a consequence of swing targets reached, not reached, or exceeded. If, for example, the Trident target is not reached, then the next target may be exceeded in order to balance the two swings. Likewise, if the last two targets were not reached then the third swing target would have to be exceeded by an extent equal to the previous failures in order to bring about the balance. There exists unique formulas which define the proper balance price for each swing, dependent upon the number of swings to be balanced (1, 2, 3, 4 . . . etc.).

The swing prices $P_1$, $P_2$, $P_3$, . . . , etc., exists as market facts. The actual balance between buying and selling pressure occurred at a corresponding swing price. But then why does a swing terminate at a particular price? Can that price be predicted? According to the Trident algorithm the target (T) represents the single swing balance moving from $P_3$ to $P_4$. However, Trident targets do not correspond to actual market prices frequently enough to assume that the target (T) is a true balance price for the market at that moment. Therefore, the target (T) is only significant as some lower level balance which functions as a reference for sequential adjustments relative to the real balancing occurring from swing to swing in the market.

In order to develop a general equation which expresses a swing price level that will balance 1, 2, . . . , 5, 6, . . . , etc., swings, it is necessary to examine the initial balance price between several swings. Consider the swing $P_2$ to $P_3$; at the moment $P_3$ is formed, variance between $P_3$ and $T_3$ would be added to the variance between $P_2$ and $T_2$ forming net variance, or,

$$V_2 = (P_2 - T_2) + (P_3 - T_3)$$

Where $V_2$ represents the variance from two (2) targets.

The next swing $P_3$ to $P_4$ has a target (T) and a balance ($B_3$) equal to $T + V_2$. If $V_2$ (net variance) were equal to zero then the target (T) would be identical to the balance price $P_3$ or,

$$B_3 = T, \text{ if } V_2 = 0$$

If, however, $V_2$ is not equal to zero, then $B_3$ would differ from T by the net amount $V_2$. Therefore, a higher level of market balance does exist in terms of a calculated price which depends upon variances between the actual swing price and a corresponding target.

If the target (T) represents a balance price for one (1) swing ($B_1$) and $T + V_1$ ($V_1 = P_3 - T_3$) equals the balance price for two (2) swings ($B_2$), then a general equation for $B_n$ can be derived directly from the target equation:

$$T = B_1 = P_2 + P_3 - P_1$$

Let n = 1, then the equation can be written:

$$B_n = P_2 + P_2 - (n - 2) - P_2 - (n)$$

Based upon the general equation for $B_n$ the following equations are true:

$$B_0 = P_4$$
$$B_1 = P_2 + P_3 - P_1$$
$$B_2 = 2P_2 - P_0$$
$$B_3 = P_2 + P_1 - P_{-1}$$
$$B_4 = P_2 + P_0 - P_{-2}$$

Accordingly, an equation for $B_n$ can be derived which would represent the balance price for all swings developed after the first Trident formation. (Theoretically, a balance price which balances all swings since the inception of the first two (2) swings for the contract would approach $P_4$ with a startling accuracy.) Therefore, the general form of the swing balance equation can be expressed as follows:

$$\boxed{B_n = P_2 + P_{2 + (2 - n)} - P_{(2 - n)}}$$

## TREND CHANGES

The commodity trading public is incredible. They rush to buy markets at their Intermediate highs and they rush to sell markets at their Intermediate lows. Some traders and some advisory letters measure this phenomena (contrary opinion) as though an axiom exists that suggests that the public can be expected always to do the wrong thing. Yet it is true that traders tend to follow each other, creating a self-fulfilling prophecy in terms of price movement until their buying or selling power is exhausted. In spite of this, there remain a few shrewd traders who understand the principle that:

***Selling high and buying low will make you profit wherever you go.***

They seem to know instinctively that the commodity most in demand today is the hot potato that nobody wants tomorrow.

Market trend changes occur because the market becomes overbought or oversold. But the concept of overbought and oversold is nothing more than the idea of ***balance.*** The question that must be answered always is how we measure overbought or oversold. Relative to what? In other words, if the market is oversold or overbought, at what price would it be neither overbought or oversold? The question of balance must be placed in context relative to the swing level under investigation. For example, the market may be overbought relative to a subordinate swing level and oversold relative to a higher swing level.

The trend direction of a particular market is determined by the action swing of the next higher level swing. If a trader were interested in trading Minor swings, then the trend of the market is in the direction of the most current Intermediate action swing. If a trader were interested in trading Intermediate swings, then the trend direction in the market would be determined by the most current Major action swing. The trend of a market, therefore, is merely completion of the next higher level swing. Market analysis directed toward forecasting price action must include the probability of a higher level terminus formation, i.e. the trader's goal is to remain on the correct side of the market.

## BALANCE PRICES

A Commodity Market which continually fails to reach its upside target and at the same time overshoots its downside target, will, in rapid succession, reach a price of zero. A market which continually exceeds its upside target and fails to reach its downside

**Commodity:** ***SILVER DEC 1975***

| DATE | ACTUAL | TARGET | VARIANCE | $B_2$ | $B_6$ |
|---|---|---|---|---|---|
| 8/28/75 | $4.88^{5}$ | 4.85 | +.035 | 4.96 | 4.86 |
| 9/02/75 | 4.47 | 4.59 | - .11 | $4.55^{5}$ | 4.71 |
| 9/04/75 | $4.64^{5}$ | $4.60^{5}$ | +.040 | $4.72^{5}$ | $4.90^{5}$ |
| 9/09/75 | (4.39) | 4.23 | +.160 | 4.19 | 4.51 |
| 9/10/75 | 4.70 | $4.56^{5}$ | +.135 | $4.40^{5}$ | 4.56 |
| 9/11/75 | $4.58^{5}$ | $4.44^{5}$ | +.140 | 4.31 | $4.19^{5}$ |
| 9/12/75 | (4.75) | $4.89^{5}$ | -.145 | $4.75^{5}$ | 4.54 |
| 9/16/75 | 4.64 | $4.63^{5}$ | +.005 | 4.78 | $4.30^{5}$ |
| 9/16/75 | $4.72^{5}$ | $4.80^{5}$ | - .080 | 4.80 | 4.51 |
| 9/17/75 | $4.54^{5}$ | $4.61^{5}$ | - .070 | $4.69^{5}$ | 4.56 |
| 9/18/75 | 4.70 | 4.63 | +.070 | 4.70 | 4.78 |
| 9/22/75 | ($4.44^{5}$) | 4.52 | - .- 75 | 4.45 | 4.74 |
| 9/26/75 | $4.62^{5}$ | 4.60 | +.025 | $4.67^{5}$ | 4.75 |
| 9/29/75 | $4.50^{5}$ | 4.37 | +.135 | $4.34^{5}$ | 4.50 |
| 10/01/75 | $4.64^{5}$ | $4.68^{5}$ | - .040 | $4.70^{5}$ | 4.60 |
| 10/01/75 | 4.55 | $4.52^{5}$ | +.025 | $4.56^{5}$ | 4.41 |
| 10/02/75 | ($4.64^{5}$) | 4.69 | - .045 | $4.66^{5}$ | 4.62 |
| 10/03/75 | $4.41^{5}$ | 4.55 | - .135 | $4.59^{5}$ | 4.45 |
| 10/07/75 | $4.53^{5}$ | 4.51 | +.015 | $4.64^{5}$ | 4.57 |
| 10/09/75 | $4.27^{5}$ | $4.30^{5}$ | - .030 | 4.28 | $4.47^{5}$ |
| 10/10/75 | 4.39 | $4.39^{5}$ | - .005 | $4.42^{5}$ | $4.55^{5}$ |
| 10/13/75 | (4.23) | 4.13 | +.100 | $4.13^{5}$ | 4.32 |
| 10/15/75 | $4.40^{5}$ | $4.34^{5}$ | +.060 | $4.24^{5}$ | 4.39 |

Table 20. Minor Balance Price Data

target will rapidly reach the moon. Yet commodity prices never reach zero, nor do they reach the moon (very often).

Therefore, swings can be expected to alternate between target excess and target failure. Suppose a market failed to reach its last upside target. Then $B_2$ (2-swing balance price) will be above the next target by an amount equal to the previous failure. So long as $B_2$ remains above each corresponding target, the market can be thought of as short term bearish or in a short term downtrend. Imagine if $B_6$ (6-swing balance price) were above the target (T) for the next swing. Then it's axiomatic that the trend of the market is bearish and the market will have to turn upward in order to find balance. If this same hypothetical market is observed several swings later and both $B_2$ and $B_6$ were below the current market, then it would be axiomatic that a trend change has occurred. That is, the market under observation has changed from bearish to bullish. The final question is, therefore, was there an advanced signal that indicated the trend change?

An investigation of the equations for $B_2$ and $B_6$ reveals a significant fact:

$$B_2 = 2\,P_2 - P_0$$
$$B_6 = P_2 + P_{-2} - P_{-4}$$

The balance price for the next swing within a particular number of swings is dependent upon P2 and not P3. Therefore, the balance price for the swing after next can be calculated at the same time. In other words, a Trident Trader can analyze the balance price for two (2) swings in advance of the market.

Next swing: $B_2 = 2\,P_2 - P_0$
Swing after next: $B_2 = 2\,P_3 - P_1$

and,

$$\text{Next swing: } B_6 = P_2 + P_{-2} - P_{-4}$$
$$\text{Swing after next: } B_6 = P_3 + P_{-1} - P_{-3}$$

This means that the relationship between $B_2$ and $B_6$ can be analyzed several swings in advance in order to forecast trend changes.

The Minor balance price data (Table 20) indicates the following Intermediate prices:

$I_1$ 4.39
$I_2$ 4.75
$I_3$ $4.44^5$
$I_4$ $4.64^5$
$I_5$ 4.23

with Minor swings occurring along each intermediate leg. If a pattern relationship between $B_2$ and $B_6$ does exist, then a detailed analysis of $B_2$ and $B_6$ before and after the Intermediate terminus should reveal that relationship.

Observe the alternating higher-lower relationship between $B_2$ and $B_6$ (Table 21). If the Intermediate terminus is a low, then $B_6$ is above $B_2$; if, however, the Intermediate terminus is a high, then $B_2$ is above $B_6$. In other words, at the low, the longer term balance ($B_6$) is above the market and moves below the market by the time the next high is established. Similarly, the short term balance ($B_2$) is below the market at the Intermediate low and moves above the market by the time the Intermediate high is reached. This relationship between $B_2$ and $B_6$ suggests that the long term balance ($B_6$) exerts an influence on the market affecting trend direction. The short term balance ($B_2$) appears to have a subordinate influence

Commodity: *SILVER DEC 1975*

| DATE | ACTUAL | $B_2$ | $B_6$ |
|---|---|---|---|
| 9/09/75 | 4.39 | 4.19 | (4.51) |
| 9/12/75 | 4.75 | ($4.75^5$) | 4.54 |
| 9/22/75 | $4.44^5$ | 4.45 | (4.74) |
| 10/01/75 | $4.64^5$ | ($4.66^5$) | 4.62 |
| 10/13/75 | 4.23 | $4.13^5$ | (4.32) |

( ) Indicates higher balance price

Table 21. $B_2$ vs $B_6$ at Intermediate Terminus

within the range of the longer term balance.

The fact that $B_2$ and $B_6$ alternate between Intermediate highs and lows is significant. However, the significance is not in the fact, but in analysis of when the two (2) balances cross each other. Clearly, $B_6$ is above $B_2$ at the Intermediate low and $B_2$ is above $B_6$ at the Intermediate high, but upon which swing prior to the higher low did $B_2$ cross $B_6$? Consider the balance price data (Table 20); on 8/28, $B_2$ (4.96) was above $B_6$ (4.86). Upon the next swing (9/02), $B_6$ (4.71) is above $B_2$ ($4.55^5$). The next valley (4.39) after $B_2$ crossed $B_6$ terminated a downtrend. Conversely, on 9/10, $B_6$ (4.56) was above $B_2$ ($4.40^5$) and upon the next swing (9/11), $B_2$ (4.31) is above $B_6$ ($4.19^5$); the next peak (4.75), after $B_6$ crossed $B_2$, terminated an uptrend. This sequence of events can be observed consistently, which leads to the following trend change rules and conditions:

***If $B_2$ was above $B_6$ for the last swing, and $B_6$ is above $B_2$ for the current swing, then $P_3$ for the current swing will be below***

***$B_6$ and the next valley after the current swing will terminate a downtrend.***

***If $B_6$ was above $B_2$ for the last swing, and $B_2$ is above $B_6$ for the current swing, then $P_3$ for the current swing will be above $B_6$ and the next peak after the current swing will terminate an uptrend.***

The trend change rules are extremely powerful tools. Application of these rules should prevent a Trident Trader from attempting to trade the wrong side of the market and, at the same time, prevent the trader from buying markets at their high or selling markets at their low. Each Trident Trade should be screened using the trend change rules along with other trade criteria. The trader who plans carefully will discover that the Commodity Market is a gold mine with many rich veins awaiting someone to come along with the proper tools.

## TRIDENT CASE HISTORY

This section will demonstrate the sequential steps leading to successful Trident Trades including initial market analysis, calculations and broker orders. The case history is based upon Silver Dec. 1975. However, any one of more than twenty (20) actively traded commodities could have been selected. The exercise will attempt to simulate true trading conditions; the same conditions a trader may expect to encounter while trading the real market. The case history is based upon the assumption that a trader has not traded the Silver market prior to August 27, 1975, and, therefore, the trader must begin from scratch.

August 27, 1975 $4.83^3$ $4.87^5$ $4.75^0$ $4.84^5$
*evening*

The following price data was obtained from the Wall Street Journal, although *any newspaper with accurate daily commodity prices can be used:*

| DATE | OPEN | HIGH | LOW | CLOSE |
|---|---|---|---|---|
| 8/01/75 | $5.23^5$ | $5.27^5$ | $5.21^0$ | $5.26^5$ |
| 8/04/75 | $5.28^0$ | $(5.40^0)$ | $5.28^0$ | $5.33^3$ |
| 8/05/75 | $5.29^3$ | $5.32^0$ | $5.23^0$ | $5.23^5$ |
| 8/06/75 | $5.23^5$ | $5.34^5$ | $(5.21^2)$ | $5.34^0$ |
| 8/07/75 | $5.38^0$ | $((5.47^0))$ | $5.38^0$ | $5.41^0$ |
| 8/08/75 | $5.34^0$ | $5.40^0$ | $5.21^0$ | $5.21^0$ |
| 8/11/75 | $5.21^5$ | $5.21^5$ | $(5.11^5)$ | $5.16^5$ |
| 8/12/75 | $5.15^5$ | $(5.29^5)$ | $5.15^5$ | $5.24^0$ |
| 8/13/75 | $5.24^0$ | $5.26^0$ | $5.04^5$ | $5.06^2$ |
| 8/14/75 | $5.08^5$ | $5.10^5$ | $(4.94^0)$ | $5.03^5$ |
| 8/15/75 | $5.01^5$ | $(5.11^0)$ | $5.00^5$ | $5.04^0$ |
| 8/18/75 | $5.04^0$ | $5.04^0$ | $((4.90^0))$ | $5.02^7$ |
| 8/19/75 | $4.92^7$ | $5.05^0$ | $4.91^0$ | $5.40^5$ |
| 8/20/75 | $5.00^5$ | $((5.13^0))$ | $4.99^5$ | $5.00^5$ |
| 8/21/75 | $5.00^5$ | $5.05^0$ | $4.98^0$ | $4.98^0$ |
| 8/22/75 | $5.01^0$ | $5.04^0$ | $(4.94^5)$ | $5.00^5$ |
| 8/25/75 | $5.00^9$ | $(5.04^5)$ | $4.96^0$ | $5.03^5$ |
| 8/26/75 | $5.03^0$ | $5.04^0$ | $4.83^8$ | $4.85^7$ |
| 8/27/75* | $4.83^3$ | $4.87^5$ | $4.75^0$ | $4.84^5$ |

*price data obtained from the days market.

Each Minor swing high and low are ringed and analyzed. The highest Minor high and the lowest Minor low are ringed to form the current Intermediate Trident:

$$I_1\ (5.47^0),\ I_2\ (4.90^0),\ I_3\ (5.13^0)$$

Intermediate target (IT) calculated:

$$\begin{aligned} IT &= I_2 + I_3 - I_1 \\ &= 4.90^0 + 5.13^0 - 5.47^0 \\ &= \underline{4.56^0} \end{aligned}$$

The most current Minor trade is identified:

$$P_1\ (5.13^0),\ P_2\ (4.94^5),\ P_3\ (5.04^5)$$

Minor target T calculated:

$$\begin{aligned} T &= P_2 + P_3 - P_1 \\ &= 4.94^5 + 5.04^5 - 5.13^0 \\ &= \underline{4.86^0} \end{aligned}$$

*It's observed that the Minor target has been exceeded*
The short term ($B_2$) and long term ($B_6$) balance prices are calculated:

$$\begin{aligned} \textit{current}\ B_2 &= 2\ (P_2) - P_0 \\ &= 2\ (4.94^5) - 4.90^0 \\ &= \underline{4.99^0} \end{aligned}$$

*current* $B_6$ = $P_2 + P_{-2} - P_{-4}$
= $4.94^5) + 4.94^0 - 5.11^5$
= $\underline{4.77^0}$

*It's observed that both the long term and short term balance prices have been exceeded*

*next swing* $B_2$ = $2 (P_3) - P_1$
= $2 (5.04^5) - 5.13^0$
= $\underline{4.96}$

*next swing* $B_6$ = $P_3 + P_{-1} - P_{-3}$
= $5.04^5) + 5.11^0 - 5.29^5$
= $\underline{4.86^8}$

$B_2$ and $B_6$ are analyzed applying the Trend Change Rule:

| $B_2$ | $B_6$ |
|---|---|
| $4.99^0$ | $4.77^0$ |
| $4.96^0$ | $4.86^0$ |

$B_2$ is above $B_6$ for both current and next swing; downtrend will remain unchanged.

The current low ($4.75^0$) qualifies as a ringed low, peak valley qualification, i.e. $4.75^0$ is lower than the previous day's low ($4.83^8$) and the current trade is completed; target was $4.86^0$. Calculate the $P_3$ Window for the next trade to the downside:

$P_1$ ($4.94^5$), $P_2$ ($5.04^5$), $P_3$ ($4.75^0$) assumption

| | | |
|---|---|---|
| Determinate (D) | = | $.625\ (P_2 - P_1) + P_3$ |
| | = | $.625\ (5.04^5 - 4.94^5) + 4.75^0$ |
| | = | $\underline{4.81^2}$ |
| Trend Reversal (TR) | = | $.625\ (P_2 - P_3) + P_3$ |
| | = | $.625\ (5.04^5 - 4.75^0) + 4.75^0$ |
| | = | $\underline{4.93^4}$ |

*it's observed that the current price (close)* $4.84^5$ *is within the* $P_3$ *Window.* The next swing $B_2$ and $B_6$ are calculated:

| | | |
|---|---|---|
| $B_2$ | = | $2\ (P_3) - P_1$ |
| | = | $2\ (4.75^0) - 4.94^5$ |
| | = | $\underline{4.55^5}$ |
| $B_6$ | = | $P_3 + P_{-1} - P_{-3}$ |
| | = | $4.75^0 + 4.90^0 - 4.94^0$ |
| | = | $\underline{4.71^0}$ |

$B_2$ will move below $B_6$ at the next low, which means that the downtrend will change upon the next low after the new trade currently forming, based on the ***Trend Change Rule.***

| $B_2$ | $B_6$ |
|---|---|
| $4.96^0$ | $4.86^0$ |
| $4.55^0$ | $4.71^0$ |

A new $P_3$ is expected to form above $4.87^5$, ***Peak Valley Qualification Test,*** and below $4.93^4$, ***$P_3$ Window limit.*** Confirmation of a new $P_3$ will occur upon an Entry Differential of:

$$ED = (P3 - P2) \div 4$$
$$= (4.75^0 - 5.04^5) \div 4$$
$$= \underline{.074}$$

*actual calculation .0737 and rounded in favor of confirmation.* The market analysis can be summarized as follows:

| Intermediate Trident | | | IT | Minor Trident | | | $B_2$ | $B_6$ | $P_3$Window | Entry Diff |
|---|---|---|---|---|---|---|---|---|---|---|
| $I_1$ | $I_2$ | $I_3$ | $4.56^0$ | $P_1$ | $P_2$ | $P_3$ | $4.96^0$ | $4.86^0$ | $4.81^2 - 4.93^4$ | -.074 |
| $5.47^0$ | $4.90^0$ | $5.13^0$ | | $4.94^5$ | $5.04^5$ | $4.75^0$ | $4.55^5$ | $4.71^0$ | | |

*the information summarized above could have been obtained within a few minutes after the daily price statistics were obtained — note the wealth of information available before a trade is made.*

**August 28, 1975** $4.87^7$ $4.88^5$ $4.76^0$ $4.77^2$
*morning*

7 a.m. a broker order is given

***SELL DEC SILVER UPON ANY PULL BACK OF 7.4¢ FROM THE HIGHEST PRICE REACHED. DO NOT PLACE ORDER IF MARKET MOVES ABOVE 4.93⁴.***

*the market opened at $4.87^7$; rose to $4.88^5$ and moved downward for the remainder of the trading session.*
Based upon broker information, the following Information Line is calculated:

| Trident Prices | | | Target Price | Critical Price | Entry Price | Profit Amount | Stop Protected | Stop Differential | Risk Amount |
|---|---|---|---|---|---|---|---|---|---|
| $P_1$ | $P_2$ | $P_3$ | | | | | | | |
| $5.04^5$ | $4.75^0$ | $4.88^5$ | $4.59^0$ | $4.73^7$ | $4.81^0$ | $1,106 | $4.88^6$ | .033 | $375 |

*observe that the Minor target does not exceed the Intermediate target.*

A specific broker order is given:

***SELL STOP DEC SILVER 4.81⁰***
***OBJECTIVE 4.59⁰***
***PROTECTIVE STOP 4.88⁶***

*the trade is executed at approximately $4.81^0$ depending upon execution on the trading floor.*
By the close of market the trade is in profit by $190.00. The market closes at $4.77^2$.

**August 29, 1975** $4.75^7$ $4.76^5$ $4.63^5$ $4.66^0$
*morning*

The Window ($4.74^9$) is entered shortly after the market opens; a broker order is given:

***CANCEL PROTECTIVE STOP $4.88^6$***
***OFFSET SILVER TRADE UPON ANY RALLY OF 3.3¢ FROM THE LOWEST PRICE REACHED OR $4.59^0$ OCO.***

The market moves down to $4.63^5$ and closes at $4.66^0$ without a rally in excess of 3.3¢ from the lowest price reached. Profit in progress: $750.00.

**September 2, 1975** 4.48$^0$ 4.51$^5$ 4.47$^0$ 4.47$^0$
*morning*

The market opens at 4.48$^0$ well below the offset objective of 4.59$^0$. The trade is immediately offset at 4.49$^0$, *the average assumed execution price.* Trade profit:

| | | |
|---|---|---|
| Sell Price | = | 4.81$^0$ |
| Buy Price | = | 4.49$^0$ |
| | = | $.32 X 5000 oz = $1600.00 |

**September 3, 1975** 4.55$^0$ 4.60$^0$ 4.52$^8$ 4.59$^2$
*evening*

The market has already moved below the Intermediate target (4.56$^0$) and therefore cannot be traded to the downside. Current Trident is:

$P_1$ (4.75$^0$), $P_2$ (4.88$^5$), $P_3$ (4.47$^0$)

*even though a trade to the downside will not be taken, the market analysis Information Line should be completed.*

The new $P_3$ Window is:

$$D = .625\,(P_2 - P_1) + P_3$$
$$= .625\,(4.88^5 - 4.75^0) + 4.47^0$$
$$= \underline{4.55^4}$$

$$
\begin{aligned}
TR &= .625\,(P_2 - P_3) + P_3 \\
&= .625\,(4.88^5 - 4.47^0) + 4.47^0 \\
&= \underline{4.72^9}
\end{aligned}
$$

Long and short term balance prices for the next two swings are:

$$
\begin{aligned}
B_2 &= 2\,(P_2) - P_0 \\
&= 2\,(4.88^5) - 5.04^5 \\
&= \underline{4.72^5}
\end{aligned}
$$

$$
\begin{aligned}
B_6 &= P_2 + P_{-2} - P_{-4} \\
&= 4.88^5 + 5.13^0 - 5.11 \\
&= \underline{4.90^5}
\end{aligned}
$$

$$
\begin{aligned}
B_2 &= 2\,(P_3) - P_1 \\
&= 2\,(4.47) - 4.75^0 \\
&= \underline{4.19^0}
\end{aligned}
$$

$$
\begin{aligned}
B_6 &= P_3 + P_{-1} - P_3 \\
&= 4.47^0 + 4.94^5 - 4.90^0 \\
&= \underline{4.51^5}
\end{aligned}
$$

Entry Differential is:

$$
\begin{aligned}
ED &= (P_3 - P_2) \div 4 \\
&= (4.47 - 4.88^5) \div 4 \\
&= \underline{-.104}
\end{aligned}
$$

Current market analysis is summarized as follows:

| Intermediate Trident | | | IT | Minor Trident | | | $B_2$ | $B_6$ | $P_3$ Window | Entry Diff |
|---|---|---|---|---|---|---|---|---|---|---|
| $I_1$ | $I_2$ | $I_3$ | | $P_1$ | $P_2$ | $P_2$ | | | | |
| $5.47^0$ | $4.90^0$ | $5.13^0$ | $4.56^0$ | $4.75^0$ | $4.88^5$ | $4.47^0$ | $4.72^5$ $4.19^0$ | $4.90^5$ $4.51^5$ | $4.55^4 - 4.72^9$ | -.104 |

*observe that B6 is above B2 for both swings, which confirms that the longer term balance is well above the market and therefore a trend change is imminent. But then, this was known before the last trade was taken. It is significant that the Minor target will exceed the Intermediate target, provided a new P3 does not form above $4.97^5$; and B6 is above B2, implying a trend change. The next trade to the downside should not reach its target and the trade should not be taken.*

**September 4, 1975** $4.64^0$ $4.64^5$ $4.53^5$ $4.61^0$
*evening*

The day's market confirmed a new P3 ($4.64^5$) which was well within the P3 Window. Had the trade been taken, entry would have been:

$$4.64^5 - .104 = 4.54^1$$

and a *loss in progress* basis the close (4.610) of $345.00. The new Trident is:

P1 ($4.88^5$), P2 ($4.47^0$), P3 ($4.64^5$)

**September 5, 1975** $4.59^3$ $4.61^5$ $4.56^0$ $4.61^0$
*evening*

The day's market traded in a narrow trading range (5.5¢) establishing no new rings (high or low). Had a trade been taken, the loss in progress would continue to be \$345.00 basis the close ($4.61^0$).

**September 8, 1975** $4.58^5$ $4.58^5$ $4.53^0$ $4.53^0$
*evening*

A new ringed low is imminent, based on the ***Peak-Valley Qualification Test.*** If the market moves higher during the next session, then a new P3 could form. However, the Trend Change Rule states that this current downswing will terminate the downtrend. Therefore, a low lower than $4.47^0$ can be expected. *Any rally greater than* $(4.64^5 - 4.47^0) \div 4 = 4.4$*¢, after the market has moved below* $4.47^0$ *would signal the new Intermediate low. Confirmation would occur upon a rally of:* $(5.13^0 - 4.90^0) \div 4 = 5.75$*¢.*

**September 9, 1975** $4.54^0$ $4.67^0$ $4.39^0$ $4.60^0$
*evening*

A new Intermediate low was established ***(assumption based upon Trend Change Rule).***

$I_1$ ($4.90^0$), $I_2$ ($5.13^0$), $I_3$ ($4.39^0$)

The new Intermediate target is:

$$\begin{aligned} IT &= I_2 + I_3 - I_1 \\ &= 5.13^0 + 4.39^0 - 4.90^0 \\ &= \underline{4.62^0} \end{aligned}$$

Based upon the Intermediate Trident, the next Intermediate swing should be an ***Intermediate reaction swing,*** provided $I_3$ ($4.39^0$) is not a major level low ($M_3$). The $I_3$ Window is: $5.13^1$

$$
\begin{aligned}
ID &= .625\,(I_2 - I_1) + I_3 \\
&= .625\,(5.13^0 - 4.90^0) + 4.39^0 \\
&= \underline{4.53^3}
\end{aligned}
$$

$$
\begin{aligned}
ITR &= .625\,(I_2 - I_3) + I_3 \\
&= .625\,(5.13^0 - 4.39^0) + 4.39^0 \\
&= \underline{4.85^2}
\end{aligned}
$$

The next Minor trade will be to the upside. But, the Intermediate target has already been reached and exceeded. Therefore, the Intermediate reaction swing does not represent a good trading opportunity. *Intermediate reaction swings often represent Minor trading opportunities, depending upon analysis of Minor target vs Intermediate target.*

The new Minor Trident is:

$$P_1\,(4.47^0),\ P_2\,(4.64^5),\ P_3\,(4.39^0)$$

with short and long term balances for the next two swings:

$$
\begin{aligned}
B_2 &= 2\,(P_2) - P_0 \\
&= 2\,(4.64^5) - 4.88^5 \\
&= \underline{4.40^5}
\end{aligned}
$$

$$
\begin{aligned}
B_6 &= P_2 + P_{-2} - P_{-4} \\
&= 4.64^5 + 5.04^5 - 5.13^0 \\
&= \underline{4.56^0}
\end{aligned}
$$

$$B_2 = 2(P_3) - P_1 = 2(4.39^0) - 4.47^0 = \underline{4.31^0}$$

$$B_6 = P_3 + P_{-1} - P_{-3} = 4.39^0 + 4.75^0 - 4.94^5 = \underline{4.15^5}$$

*Observe that P3 = I3 and therefore the current Minor swing will be the first Minor action swing in an upward direction. The P3 Window and Entry Differential have no significance because no trade to the downside is contemplated. However, the market analysis summary should be completed.*

The P3 Window is:

$$D = .625(P_2 - P_1) + P_3 = .625(4.64^5 - 4.47^0) + 4.39^0 = \underline{4.50^0}$$

$$TR = .625(P_2 - P_3) + P_3 = .625(4.64^5 - 4.47^0) + 4.39^0 = \underline{4.55^0}$$

*note that the market has already moved beyond the P3 Window (4.67^0 vs 4.55^0) confirming the trend change.*

The Entry Differential is:

$$\begin{aligned} ED &= (P_3 - P_2) \div 4 \\ &= (4.39^0 - 4.64^5) \div 4 \\ &= \underline{-.063} \end{aligned}$$

The market analysis results in the following summary:

| Intermediate Trident | | | IT | Minor Trident | | | $B_2$ | $B_6$ | $P_3$ Window | Entry Diff |
|---|---|---|---|---|---|---|---|---|---|---|
| $I_1$ | $I_2$ | $I_3$ | | $P_1$ | $P_2$ | $P_3$ | $4.40^5$ | $4.56^0$ | $4.50^0 - 4.55^0$ | -.063 |
| $4.90^0$ | $5.13^0$ | $4.39^0$ | $4.62^0$ | $4.47^0$ | $4.62^5$ | $4.39^0$ | $4.31^0$ | $4.19^5$ | | |

Analysis of the market summary reveals an upcoming trend change. $B_2$ ($4.31^0$) moves above $B_6$ ($4.19^5$) at the next low, which means that the peak after next will terminate the Intermediate reaction swing. *In other words, there should be two action swings to the upside before the Intermediate move ends.*

**September 10, 1975** $4.66^2$ $4.70^0$ $4.61^5$ $4.66^0$
*evening*

New $P_3$ formed ($4.70^0$) ***Peak Valley Qualification*** confirmed by a pullback of -.063, or $4.70^0 - .063 = 4.63^7$. The new Minor Trident is:

$P_1$ ($4.64^5$), $P_2$ ($4.39^0$), $P_3$ ($4.70^0$)

*Note that the swing $P_1$ ($4.64^5$) to $P_2$ ($4.39^0$) is the last action swing completing the Intermediate leg, $5.13^0$ to $4.39^0$. The Swing $P_2$ ($4.39^0$) to $P_3$ ($4.70^0$) is the first swing along a new Intermediate reaction swing. Both swings are Minor action swings, and, therefore, the $P_3$ Window must be calculated using the $P_3$ Window exception equation.*

The P3 Window is:

$$D = .625\,(P_0 - P_1) + P_3$$
$$= .625\,(4.47^0 - 4.64^5) + 4.70^0$$
$$= \underline{4.59^0}$$

$$TR = .625\,(P_2 - P_3) + P_3$$
$$= .625\,(4.39^0 - 4.70^0)$$
$$= \underline{4.50^6}$$

The Entry Differential is:

$$ED = (P_3 - P_2) \div 4$$
$$= (4.70^0 - 4.39^5) \div 4$$
$$= \underline{.07^7}$$

*If a valid P3 forms within the P3 Window, the trade should not be taken because the Intermediate target to the upside has already been exceeded ($4.62^0$ vs $4.67^0$).*

**September 11, 1975** $4.62^0$ $4.65^0$ $4.58^5$ $4.61^5$
*evening*

A new P3 may have formed today ($4.58^5$). However, confirmation requires a rally of $.07^7$ or $4.66^2$. We will have to wait until the next market session.

**September 12, 1975** $4.65^0$ $4.75^0$ $4.65^0$ $4.72^3$
*morning*

Market confirms new P3 from previous day ($4.58^5$). The session also confirms a P3 Minor high ($4.75^0$) which should be the Intermediate reaction swing terminus I3. ***(These assumptions are based upon Peak Valley Qualification Tests and the Trend Change Rule.)*** However, confirmation of a new I3 requires a pull back equal to:

$$(4.39^0 - 5.13^0) \div 4 = .185 \text{ or } 4.56^5$$

The new Minor Trident is:

$$P1\ (4.70^0),\ P2\ (4.58^5),\ P3\ (4.75^0)$$

The P3 Window is:

$$\begin{aligned} D &= .625\ (P2 - P1) + P3 \\ &= .625\ (4.58^5 - 4.70^0) + 4.75^0 \\ &= \underline{4.67}^8 \end{aligned}$$

$$\begin{aligned} TR &= .625\ (P2 - P3) + P3 \\ &= .625\ (4.58^0 - 4.75^0) + 4.75^0 \\ &= \underline{4.64}^6 \end{aligned}$$

Entry Differential is:

$$\begin{aligned} ED &= (P3 - P2) \div 4 \\ &= (4.75^0 - 4.58^0) \div 4 \\ &= \underline{.041} \end{aligned}$$

**September 15, 1975** $4.70^0$ $4.72^0$ $4.68^5$ $4.70^0$
*evening*

The day's market session confirmed the Minor high, $4.75^0$. Still awaiting confirmation of Intermediate terminus ($4.75^0$). However, based upon the Trend Change Rule, $4.75^0$ will be the Intermediate high $I_3$. Therefore, the new Intermediate Trident is:

$$I_1\ (5.13^0),\ I_2\ (4.39^0),\ I_3\ (4.75^0)$$

The new IT is:

$$\begin{aligned} IT &= I_2 + I_3 - I_1 \\ &= 4.39^0 + 4.75^0 - 5.13^0 \\ &= \underline{4.01}^0 \end{aligned}$$

The short and long term balances are:

$$\begin{aligned} B_2 &= 2\,(P_2) - P_0 \\ &= 2\,(4.58^5) - 4.39^0 \\ &= \underline{4.78}^0 \end{aligned}$$

$$\begin{aligned} B_6 &= P_2 + P_{-2} - P_{-4} \\ &= 4.58^5 + 4.47^0 - 4.75^0 \\ &= \underline{4.30}^5 \end{aligned}$$

$$\begin{aligned} B_2 &= 2\,(P_3) - P_1 \\ &= 2\,(4.75^0) - 4.70^0 \\ &= \underline{4.80}^0 \end{aligned}$$

$$\begin{aligned} B_6 &= P_3 + P_{-1} - P_{-3} \\ &= 4.75^0 + 4.64^5 - 4.88^5 \\ &= \underline{4.51}^0 \end{aligned}$$

The new market analysis summary is:

| Intermediate Trident | | | IT | Minor Trident | | | $B_2$ | $B_6$ | $P_3$ Window | Entry Diff |
|---|---|---|---|---|---|---|---|---|---|---|
| $I_1$ | $I_2$ | $I_3$ | $4.01^0$ | $P_1$ | $P_2$ | $P_3$ | $4.78^0$ | $4.30^5$ | $4.67^8 - 4.64^6$ | .041 |
| $5.13^0$ | $4.39^0$ | $4.75^0$ | | $4.70^0$ | $4.58^5$ | $4.75^0$ | $4.80^0$ | $4.51^0$ | | |

$B_2$ is above $B_6$ and remains above $B_6$ for the next two swings, which means that a trend change has occurred and this market should be traded on the short side. This is confirmed by a new $I_3$ ($4.75^0$) and the IT ($4.01^0$). (Actual market confirmation will not occur until the market dips below $4.56^5$.)

**September 16, 1975** $4.66^3$ $4.72^5$ $4.64^0$ $4.64^5$
*morning*

The market opened low ($4.66^3$), penetrating the $P_3$ Window ($4.67_8$), which means that any rally of .041 will establish a new $P_3$. This, in fact, happened after the market moved down to $4.64^0$ ***(the low of the day).*** Upon confirmation of a new $P_3$, the Minor Trident is:

$$P_1\ (4.58^5),\ P_2\ (4.75^0),\ P_3\ (4.64^0)$$

*Note that $P_2$ ($4.75^0$) is assumed to be $I_3$ which means that the swing, $P_1$ ($4.58^5$) to $P_2$ ($4.75^0$), is the last Minor action swing along the Intermediate leg, $4.39^0$ to $4.75^0$. Also, based upon the same assumption, the swing $P_2$ ($4.75^0$) to $P_3$ ($4.64^0$) is the first Minor action swing in the new down direction. The $P_3$ Window Exception Rule will have to be applied.*

The $P_3$ Window is:

$$
\begin{aligned}
D &= .625\,(P_0 - P_1) + P_3 \\
&= .625\,(4.70^0 - 4.58^5) + 4.64^0 \\
&= \underline{4.71^2}
\end{aligned}
$$

$$
\begin{aligned}
TR &= .625\,(P_2 - P_3) + P_3 \\
&= .625\,(4.75^0 - 4.64^0) + 4.64^0 \\
&= \underline{4.70^8}
\end{aligned}
$$

The Entry Differential is:

$$
\begin{aligned}
ED &= (P_3 - P_2) \div 4 \\
&= (4.64^0 - 4.75^0) \div 4 \\
&= \underline{.028}
\end{aligned}
$$

*Note that the $P_3$ Window is inverted, i.e. the Determinate (D) is above the Trend Reversal price (TR). $P_3$ Window Inversion occurs because the $P_3$ ($4.64^0$) is above $P_1$ ($4.58^5$) and the Trident resembles a normal action - reaction pattern. However, there are two (2) consecutive Minor action swings. In other words, the $P_3$ Window begins at D ($4.71^2$) but does not appear to have an upper boundary. If a new $P_3$ were to form above $4.75^0$, then the assumption that $4.75^0$ is $I_3$ is false. Therefore, $4.75^0$ becomes the upper limit of the $P_3$ Window — see Chapter 7, ($P_3$ Window).*

When the market moves into the $P_3$ Window, $4.71^2$, a broker order is given:

***SELL DEC SILVER UPON A PULL BACK OF 2.8¢ FROM THE HIGHEST PRICE REACHED. DO NOT***

***PLACE ORDER IF MARKET MOVES ABOVE 4.75.***

Based upon broker information the following Information Line was calculated:

| Trident Prices | | | Target Price | Critical Price | Entry Price | Profit Amount | Stop Protected | Stop Differential | Risk Amount |
|---|---|---|---|---|---|---|---|---|---|
| $P_1$ | $P_2$ | $P_3$ | | | | | | | |
| $4.75^0$ | $4.64^0$ | $4.72^5$ | $4.61^5$ | $4.67^0$ | $4.69^7$ | $410.00 | $4.72^6$ | .021 | $140 |

A specific broker order was given:

***SELL DEC SILVER $4.69^7$ STOP***
***OBJECTIVE $4.61^5$***
***PROTECTIVE STOP $4.72^6$***

During the trading session, the market reached the critical price ($4.67^0$). Another broker order was given:

***CANCEL PROTECTIVE STOP $4.72^6$; PLACE NEW PROTECTIVE STOP $4.69^7$***

The market closed with profit in progress of $260.00.

**September 17, 1975** $4.59^5$ $4.70^0$ $4.54^5$ $4.69^2$
*morning*

The trade was offset at the market open, since the opening price ($4.59^5$) was below the trade objective ($4.61^5$). The trade profit was:

$$(4.69^7 - 4.59^5) = 10.2¢ \text{ X } 5000 \text{ oz} = \$510.00$$

## CONCLUSION

The two trades (8/28/75 and 9/16/75) took place over a period of approximately 2 1/2 weeks, ten (10) trading sessions; and made a total profit of $1,600 + $510.00, or $2,110. Several trades were deliberately not taken because they did not meet the trade selection criteria. Perhaps the most significant result was the way in which the Trend Change Rule signaled the formation of Intermediate highs and lows. The calculations were simple and straightforward and required only a few minutes in the evening or in the morning, depending upon whether or not a trade was in progress or imminent. ($2,110.00 was good profit for the amount of effort required.)

## SUMMARY

The complete Trident Strategy includes calculations, broker orders, trade management, trend analysis and accurate data collection. Each function is objective and to a great degree mechanical, but what can be said about the Trident Trader? Is there a particular attitude that is more conducive to success? Because no matter how good the Trident Strategy may be, the system depends upon the trader for execution. (Experienced traders have had early success with Trident, only to freeze mentally, as if the success was more than they could handle.)

A Trident Trader's attitude should be positive and business-like. It is necessary for the trader to realize that trading commodities is a business. The commodity trading business requires work and a degree of skill. The work is of an analytical nature, similar to many other planning functions. The skill is the ability to apply tools to the market with the full knowledge of what the tool does and why it must be used.

There are many traders who believe that trading commodities is simply gambling, and success or failure hinges upon luck. There is no luck involved in a market situation where the trend has definitely changed and the trader is holding on to a trade going the wrong way. Some commodity traders believe that the market is out to get their money and are mildly paranoid. Still other commodity traders develop attachments to certain markets while avoiding other markets, depending upon whether or not that market has been "nice" to them. All Commodity Markets and all trades within those markets are the same. Just like any other business, the customer (commodity contract) will respond to positive treatment (qualified trades).

Commodity trading requires patience and emotional control. Traders in local Brokerage Houses can be seen rushing to place new trades and rushing to offset old trades in a near state of panic, as if their very life depends upon speed of execution (sometimes panic is justified due to pending financial disaster). Accurate Trident calculations made under emotional stress are somewhat unreliable, if not impossible. A businessman knows that one customer (trade) will not make or break him. Therefore, the businessman develops a consistent approach (strategy) designed to satisfy the needs of his business (the market). Self control is the necessary discipline for consistent positive market results.

The Trident Trader should remain always a student of the market. The earliest price action theorists suggested that ***there is no problem in the market that cannot be solved.*** This statement was made over fifty (50) years ago at a time when accurate price information was difficult to come by, yet, as it was true then, it's doubly true today. The market contains many mysteries; such as inverses, shadows, echoes, Fibanacci series and many other observable phenomena, some of which are so secret that they cannot be mentioned in this book. Yet, each swing terminus can be calculated exactly after they have formed. The problem is simple - there has not been sufficient research to discover the single equation that defines immediate balance. Therefore, only through becoming a student of the market can a Trident Trader remain sufficiently open to continue to learn new ideas, new theories, and new solutions to mysteries of the market.

Each market day is a new opportunity to apply Trident Strategy. The opportunity is two-fold: first the opportunity to enter a new trade which most probably will make money; second, an opportunity to gain greater skill in the application of the strategy. The thrill of making money is directly proportional to the risk and challenges associated with the win. If, for example, there is no challenge and no risk, then the trader will soon become bored and disgruntled because this trade or that trade did not make as much money as some other trade. It is difficult to imagine that this can be true. Yet, how does the Blackjack player feel who has been playing Blackjack for years with a winning system that always produces profit after four hours of continuous play? Those who have been asked have openly admitted that "it's boring as hell." The Commodity Market, on the other hand, is alive and ripe with opportunity and challenge each and every day.

Accuracy is the opposite of sloppy. The Commodity Market hinges upon exact balance, not "almost" or "nearly" or "just about." A prospective trade has either reached Entry or it has not, the Window has either been entered or not, the Intermediate target either exceeds the Minor target or not. Precision is a good work habit. There can be no skill without precision and there can be no skill without practice. Therefore, accuracy must be practiced on a daily basis until the habit has been formed. Jumping the gun is sloppy. No matter how certain a trader may be that a Trident event is imminent, it is necessary to be patient enough to allow the event to happen before any attending actions are taken.

Profitable trading results from a balance between careful planning and skillful execution. Trident Strategy provides a great basis for both planning and execution. Care and skill must be provided by you, the trader. And for those traders who care enough to master this strategy, there can be nothing but overwhelming financial success and satisfaction. (And you can take it to the bank.)

# APPENDIX

## WHICH MARKETS SHOULD I TRADE?

*Answer:*

There are approximately twenty (20) active commodity markets. These twenty (20) markets differ in two principle ways:

(1) Markets differ in open interest.

(2) Markets differ in price volatility.

The basis for market selection is a function of the differences among the various markets. A simple rule of thumb would be:

"TRADE THE MARKET WITH THE GREATEST OPEN INTEREST AND THE GREATEST VOLATILITY"

*Discussion:*

In order for this rule to become operational, several other considerations must be discussed. Such things as margin, last trading day, and daily trading limit affect the rule. The trading margin (the amount of money required to buy or sell one contract option) could exceed the total capital in the trading account. The margin may commit too much of the total trading capital. The last day for trading the contract may be too near to successfully conclude the trade. Delivery intentions could become a problem. The daily trading limit could be too high and the trading account could not withstand maximum adverse fluctuation.

Commodity trading is a matter of following a sound plan which contains disciplined trading strategy and reasonable money management. Trident trading strategy satisfies the trading discipline but not much has been said about money management. There are five (5) basic commodity groups: grains, meats, metals, financials and miscellaneous. If all of the trading capital were committed to a single complex, then no new trading opportunities could be considered in the other complexes. Conversely, if a complex is essentially inactive then capital reserved for that complex would be wasted. On the other hand, a trader should not place all his trading capital at risk at the same time. Many commodity money managers believe that a trader should risk only half of his capital at any given time. What is needed, therefore, is a basic money management plan which incorporates those ideas while allowing the trader to constantly look for the best trading opportunity.

Consider the following money management plan:

1. Commit 62.5% of total trading capital to entire commodity market.
2. Assign 50% of the committed capital to the most active commodity complex.
3. Assign 30% of the committed capital to the second most active complex.
4. Assign 10% of the committed capital to the third most active complex.
5. Assign 10% of the committed capital to the fourth most active complex.
6. Assign no capital to the least active complex.
7. Look for trades in any commodity (consistent with capital) whose daily trading range exceeds $400. (That is, the difference between the daily high and daily low exceeds $400).
8. Review the five commodity complexes weekly for changes in activity (open interest and price volatility).

The advantages of this plan are threefold: (1) 37.5% of total trading capital remains in perpetual reserve, which increases chances for profit retention. (2) Concentrates trading activity in those markets which have the greatest profit potential; and (3) provides a simple technique for total market review.

The question, therefore: "Which markets should I trade?" can only be answered as a function of a total trading plan. All markets can and will produce excellent profits if there is enough trader interest and enough volatility.

## HOW MUCH CAPITAL DO I NEED TO TRADE TRIDENT?

*Answer:*

$15,000 more or less.

*Discussion:*

Each actively traded commodity requires initial trading margin which represents a modest percentage (10% - 20%) of total cost of the contracted commodity. Using Trident trading strategy, commodity markets are traded during action swings and are not traded during reaction swings. Furthermore, all action swings are not tradeable if the action swing does not meet trade selection criteria. If a trader sought to seek trades in twenty (20) active markets and wanted to be able to trade at least one contract per market then that trader would need approximately one-third of the total margin requirement for all twenty markets. Since margin requirements change, this amount will vary.

The money management plan previously discussed requires a 37.5 percent perpetual reserve. The plan also eliminates the least active commodity complex, which eliminates approximately four (4) markets. In addition, the money management plan automatically assigns and proportions the available capital so as to set or fix the number of contract units per trade. Assume the average contract margin cost to be $2,000 ($1,500 if high margined markets are eliminated). Then the amount of trading capital required would be:

(1/3 no. of markets X avg. margin) X Reserve factor.

where:

No. of markets = 20 - 4 = 16

Avg. margin = $2000

then:

Theoretical capital would be:

$$C = \frac{(16 \times 2000)}{3} \times 1.375$$

$$\boxed{C = \$14,667}$$

In round numbers, a trader needs $15,000 to trade Trident so as to take advantage of all active markets. If a trader did not have this amount of capital then what should be done? This is not a big problem because a trader could: restrict trading to one or two commodity groups; trade the lower margined, small contract Mid-America Exchange, or adapt an alternate money management strategy consistent with the amount of capital available.

Some commodity brokerage companies will establish policies which set a particular minimum account required to trade. Such minimums are in the range of $5,000 to $20,000. However, there are other brokerage firms which simply require enough capital to meet the initial margin requirement for the commodity traded. Therefore, the answer to this question is:

$15,000 more or less.

## IF I MISS TRADE ENTRY, CAN I STILL TAKE THE TRADE?

*Answer:*

Trident trade entry is a calculated price based upon a 25% retracement of the previous action swing. The Trident entry price represents the earliest price level at which a new action swing can be assumed. A trader who buys or sells a commodity at the Trident entry price reduces trade risk to a minimum. The consequences of entering a trade after it is in progress is to reduce the profit potential represented by the trade. Given these negative consequences, the trade should not be taken.

*Discussion:*

Trident entry prices represent an arbitrary price level at which a new action swing can be assumed to be in progress. There are other entry price ideas which have as much validity as the 25% standard. Consider the concept of trend reversal price. This price is defined as a price just beyond (1 tick) 62.5% retracement of the previously completed action swing. Trend reversal price is a function of an action swing, but what if the trend reversal price concept were applied to the previous "reaction swing?" How would entry based upon 62.5% retracement of the reaction swing compare with the standard Trident entry price.

Based upon the data contained in Table 1A, the following entry comparison chart was developed (Table 2A).

Commodity: Soybeans May 1977

| DATE | OPEN | HIGH | LOW | CLOSE |
|---|---|---|---|---|
| 9-03-76 | 7.170 | 7.310 | 7.170 | 7.310 |
| 9-07-76 | 7.510 | 7.510 | 7.510 | 7.510 |
| 9-08-76 | 7.710 | (7.710)[1] | 7.350 | 7.400 |
| 9-09-76 | 7.380 | 7.525 | (7.350)[2] | 7.500 |
| 9-10-76 | 7.580 | (7.580)[3] | 7.440 | 7.445 |
| 9-13-76 | 7.390 | 7.410 | 7.245 | 7.245 |
| 9-14-76 | 7.160 | 7.275 | 7.045 | 7.045 |
| 9-15-76 | 7.100 | 7.120 | (6.845)[4] | 6.960 |
| 9-16-76 | 7.010 | (7.080)[5] | 6.980 | 6.983 |
| 9-17-76 | 6.990 | 6.990 | 6.783 | 6.783 |
| 9-20-76 | 6.650 | 6.690 | (6.583)[6] | 6.630 |
| 9-21-76 | 6.700 | (6.730)[7] | 6.540 | 6.580 |
| 9-22-76 | 6.533 | 6.610 | 6.480 | 6.575 |
| 9-23-76 | 6.460 | (6.700)[9] | (6.420)[8] | 6.663 |
| 9-24-76 | 6.640 | 6.665 | 6.515 | 6538 |
| 9-27-76 | 6.520 | 6.560 | (6.375)[10] | 6.448 |
| 9-28-76 | 6.500 | (6.585)[11] | 6.435 | 6.558 |
| 9-29-76 | 6.530 | 6.545 | 6.370 | 6.375 |
| 9-30-76 | 6.360 | (6.500)[13] | (6.320)[12] | 6.495 |
| 10-01-76 | 6.490 | 6.500 | 6.360 | 6.360 |
| 10-04-76 | 6.315 | 6.560 | (6.310)[14] | 6.560 |
| 10-05-76 | 6.590 | (6.755)[15] | 6.500 | 6.600 |
| 10-06-76 | 6.590 | 6.748 | 6.580 | 6.628 |

Table 1A. Soybean Price Data

| P1 | P2 | P3 | Trident Entry | Reversal Entry | Difference | Difference Amount |
|---|---|---|---|---|---|---|
| 7.710 | 7.350 | 7.580 | 7.490 | 7.436 | .054 | $270 |
| 7.350 | 7.580 | 6.845 | | | | |
| 7.580 | 6.845 | 7.080 | 6.954 | 6.933 | .021 | $104 |
| 6.845 | 7.080 | 6.583 | | | | |
| 7.080 | 6.583 | 6.730 | 6.600 | 6.638 | .038 | ($190) |
| 6.583 | 6.730 | 6.430 | | | | |
| 6.730 | 6.420 | 6.700 | 6.620 | 6.525 | .095 | $475 |
| 6.420 | 6.700 | 6.375 | | | | |
| 6.700 | 6.375 | 6.585 | 6.503 | 6.381 | .121 | $610 |
| 6.375 | 6.585 | 6.320 | | | | |
| 6.585 | 6.320 | 6.500 | 6.430 | 6.387 | .043 | $215 |
| 6.320 | 6.500 | 6.310 | | | | |
| 6.500 | 6.310 | 6.755 | | | | |

Table 2A. Comparison between entry prices.

In the six (6) examples (Table 2A) notice that trend reversal represented a secondary entry in five (5) out of six (6) trades. Notice that in the single case where reversal entry was more advantageous than the Trident entry, the resulting trade was no better than those trades when the opposite was true. In this example, a simple conclusion can be reached, i.e. some trades represent secondary possibilities.

If a secondary entry was necessary then is there a way to reduce the large risk involved? Consider the first trade (Table 2A).

P1 (7.710), P2 (7.350), P3 (7.580)

The reversal entry is 7.436, which means that a swing (downside) has moved from 7.580 (P3) to 7.436; now, if this swing were to reverse again, then it would have to retrace .625 or:

$$.625\,(7.580 - 7.436) + 7.436 = 7.526$$

Should this market move up to 7.526 after reversal entry (7.436) was reached, then the trader would have to assume that another reversal has occurred. Notice that if this second reversal price (7.526) were used as the basis for a protective stop, then the risk of being stopped out carries the same magnitude (.090) as it would if the Trident entry had been used. Therefore, the answer to this question is complex simply because an alternate trade entry strategy must be used. Not only must an alternate entry concept come into play, but an alternate initial protective stop must be employed. If the Trident entry is missed and the trend reversal secondary entry has not been reached, and all other trade criteria have been met, then enter the trade at the secondary entry and place the initial protective stop at the next trend reversal price plus one tick. If this action were taken then all other Trident rules should be observed.

## DOES IT MATTER IF I MISS A SWING?

*Answer:*

Yes. The two swings used to establish the Trident P1, P2 and P3 must be correct. Trident strategy depends upon what the market did as a factual event. If a swing is missed and the peak-valley set would have been used in calculation, then the Trident trader's decision model will not be accurate. Whether or not a trade succeeds becomes a function of luck!

*Discussion:*

Sometimes missed swings may result in a good trade which would otherwise not pass the Trident qualification test. Consider the Soybean price data (Table 3A).

Commodity: Soybeans May 1977

| DATE | OPEN | HIGH | LOW | CLOSE |
|---|---|---|---|---|
| 9-17-76 | 6.990 | 6.990 | 6.783 | 6.783 |
| 9-20-76 | 6.650 | 6.690 | (6.583)[1] | 6.630 |
| 9-21-76 | 6.700 | (6.730)[2] | 6.540 | 6.580 |
| 9-22-76 | 6.533 | 6.610 | 6.480 | 6.575 |
| 9-23-76 | 6.460 | (6.700)[4] | (6.420)[3] | 6.663 |
| 9-24-76 | 6.640 | 6.665 | 6.515 | 6.538 |
| 9-27-76 | 6.520 | 6.560 | (6.375)[5] | 6.488 |
| 9-28-76 | 6.500 | (6.585)[6] | 6.435 | 6.558 |
| 9-29-76 | 6.530 | 6.545 | 6.370 | 6.375 |
| 9-30-76 | 6.360 | (6.500)[8] | (6.320)[7] | 6.495 |
| 10-01-76 | 6.490 | 6.500 | 6.360 | 6.360 |

Table 3A. Soybean Price Data

In this example, imagine a situation where P3 (6.420) and P4 (6.700) (9/23) were missed. On 9/27 the immediate consequence would be the Trident:

$$P_1\ (6.583),\ P_2\ (6.730),\ P_5\ (6.375)$$

the trader would calculate the $P_3$ window in anticipation of the next trade down:

$$\text{Determinate price} = .625\,(P_2 - P1) + P_3$$
$$= .625\,(6.730 - 6.583) + 6.375$$
$$= \underline{6.466}$$

$$\text{Trend reversal price} = .625\,(P_2 - P_3) + P_3$$
$$= .625\,(6.730 - 6.375) + 6.375$$
$$= \underline{6.596}$$

Observing that the price penetrates the $P_3$ window (6.560) the trader would calculate the entry differential:

$$\text{Entry} = \frac{P_2 - P_1}{4}$$

$$= \frac{\underline{6.375 - 6.730}}{4}$$

$$= \underline{-0.089}$$

On 9/28 the market moves up to 6.585 (within the $P_3$ window) and moves down the 8.9¢ (6.496) necessary to enter the trade. By 9/30 the down swing is completed and the market moves back up. The stop differential is:

$$SD = \frac{P_3 - P_2}{4}$$

$$= \frac{6.585 - 6.375}{4}$$

$$= \underline{+0.053}$$

and the trade completes at 6.372, after being stopped out by the stop differential.

Trade profit 6.496 - 6.372 x 5000 bu = \$620 per contract. Suppose, however, the swing was not missed, i.e. $P_3$ (6.420) and $P_4$ (6.700) were properly analyzed resulting in the Trident:

$P_3$ (6.420), $P_4$ (6.700), $P_5$ (6.375)

The trader would calculate the $P_3$ window:

$$\text{Determinate price} = .625\,(P_2 - P1) + P_3$$
$$= .625\,(6.700 - 6.420) + 6.375$$
$$= \underline{6.550}$$

$$\text{Trend reversal price} = .625\,(P_2 - P_3) + P_3$$
$$= .625\,(6.700 - 6.375) + 6.375$$
$$= \underline{6.578}$$

On 9/28 the trader observes that the price has broken the trend reversal price (6.585 vs 6.578) and, therefore, the trade to the downside is too risky to take.

In this example, the trader made a profit because a swing was missed, but then Trident is a trading strategy designed to consistently create a trading advantage. It is not absolute and luck is not a consideration.

## DO I REALLY NEED $B_2$ AND $B_6$?

*Answer:*

The short term (two-swing) balance price $B_2$ and the long term (six-swing) balance price $B_6$ are theoretical reference prices at which the cumulative variance between actual price and Trident target price would equal zero. Both $B_2$ and $B_6$ are zero balance prices relative to two swings and six swings respectively. Through market price action, $B_2$ could be above or below $B_6$. As the relationship between $B_2$ and $B_6$ change (above, below) then such changes are reflected in the trend direction of the market.

The trend direction of the market changes after the last minor action swing. The next swing will be the first minor action swing in the new trend direction. Most Trident losing trades occur through failure to anticipate this trend change. It is significant that several swings before the actual trend change, a change in the relationship of $B_2$ and $B_6$ would have occurred. By using this analysis, a losing trade would be eliminated. Therefore, $B_2$ and $B_6$ analysis is needed in order to avoid trade loss resulting from mistaking the first action swing in a new trend direction for a reaction swing leading to the next trade in the old trend direction.

*Discussion:*

Consider the situation where there is a change in the relationship between $B_2$ and $B_6$, but the $B_2$ and $B_6$ relationship is inverse; i.e. the $B_2$, $B_6$ switch is opposite to the trend change rule. Can trend changes be forecasted under these circumstances?

The price data (Table 5A) covers price action in Soybean Meal during the period 2-4-77 through 3-22-77. During this period there were five (5) trend changes relative to the minor swing level (Table 6A).

On 3/8 this market reached an intermediate high (249.00). Was there a change in the relationship between B2 and B6 prior to this event according to the rule:

> "If B6 was above B2 for the last swing, and B2 is above B6 for the current swing, then P3 for the current swing will be above B6 and the next peak after the current swing will terminate an uptrend."

On 3/1 B2 (229.90) was above B6 (223.30) for the last swing (230.90) down to (225.70). And B2 (235.10) is below B6 (235.70) for the current swing (P3 = 225.70). P3 for the current swing (225.70) is above B6 (223.30). But this is just opposite the trend reversal rule; i.e. this set of circumstances should apply to termination of a downtrend. An **INVERSE** has occurred in this market, which indicates that the market has just broken out of a congestion phase (narrow trading range) and will correct itself after more volatility in price action comes into the market.

The significant price action was the relative change between B2 and B6 as a signal that an intermediate terminus would form on the next peak after the current swing (225.70 to 241.00) and . . . so it did!

Observe that the **INVERSE** continues to operate until 3/23 when B2 (242.70) moves above B6 (236.10) and P3 (236.00) for the current swing is an intermediate low. Thus this market operated in an **INVERSION** mode but was able to correct itself as a result of later price action. It is this precise kind of price action that makes price action analysis a worthy and exciting pursuit.

COMMODITY: Soybean Meal July '77

| DATE | OPEN | HIGH | LOW | CLOSE |
|---|---|---|---|---|
| 2-04-77 | 209.50 | 212.00 | 209.10 | 212.00 |
| 2-07-77 | 212.00 | (215.00 | 211.50 | 212.20 |
| 2-08-77 | 211.50 | 214.00 | (210.50) | 212.90 |
| 2-09-77 | 213.00 | (214.20) | 212.40 | 213.40 |
| 2-10-77 | 213.00 | 214.00 | 212.60 | 213.10 |
| 2-11-77 | 212.80 | 213.70 | 212.50 | 213.20 |
| 2-14-77 | 213.00 | 213.20 | 212.00 | 212.30 |
| 2-15-77 | 211.00 | 212.50 | ((210.30)) | 211.30 |
| 2-16-77 | 211.00 | 214.50 | 211.00 | 214.20 |
| 2-17-77 | 215.00 | 217.80 | 215.00 | 217.60 |
| 2-18-77 | 217.00 | (219.00) | 216.80 | 218.70 |
| 2-22-77 | 217.50 | 219.00 | (217.50) | 218.30 |
| 2-23-77 | 219.00 | 226.00 | 219.00 | 224.10 |
| 2-24-77 | 223.50 | (226.70) | 223.00 | 226.30 |
| 2-25-77 | 225.00 | 226.50 | (223.70) | 225.10 |
| 2-28-77 | 226.00 | (230.90) | 226.00 | 227.70 |
| 3-01-77 | 227.50 | 229.00 | (225.70) | 228.40 |
| 3-02-77 | 229.00 | 232.30 | 229.00 | 232.10 |
| 3-03-77 | 233.50 | (241.00) | 232.50 | 240.30 |
| 3-04-77 | 239.00 | 239.80 | (237.00) | 237.90 |
| 3-07-77 | 241.00 | 246.00 | 239.50 | 242.90 |
| 3-08-77 | 247.00 | ((249.00)) | 238.00 | 239.30 |
| 3-09-77 | 239.50 | 242.00 | (236.50) | 241.00 |
| 3-10-77 | 240.50 | (242.70) | 233.50 | 235.70 |
| 3-11-77 | 237.00 | 237.00 | ((230.50)) | 234.50 |
| 3-14-77 | 234.50 | 235.90 | 231.50 | 233.80 |
| 3-15-77 | 234.00 | 236.50 | 232.80 | 233.60 |
| 3-16-77 | 234.50 | 241.50 | 234.50 | 241.40 |
| 3-17-77 | 242.50 | ((246.50)) | 237.00 | 238.20 |
| 3-18-77 | 238.20 | 241.00 | (236.60) | 239.60 |
| 3-21-77 | 239.50 | (243.50) | 239.50 | 242.30 |
| 3-22-77 | 241.00 | 241.00 | 238.20 | 239.40 |
| 3-23-77 | 241.50 | 244.50 | ((236.00)) | 239.80 |
| 3-24-77 | 238.00 | 240.00 | 237.00 | 239.60 |

Table 5A.

| DATE | SWING PRICE | $B_2$ | $B_6$ |
|---|---|---|---|
| 2-07-77 | 215.00 | | |
| 2-08-77 | 210.70 | | |
| 2-09-77 | 214.20 | | |
| 2-15-77 | (210.30)* | | |
| 2-18-77 | 219.00 | | |
| 2-22-77 | 217.50 | | |
| 2-24-77 | 226.70 | | |
| 2-25-77 | 223.70 | | |
| 2-28-77 | 230.90 | 234.40 | 225.90 |
| 3-01-77 | 225.70 | 229.90 | 223.30 |
| 3-03-77 | 241.00 | 235.10 | 235.70 |
| 3-04-77 | 237.00 | 227.70 | 232.90 |
| 3-08-77 | (249.00) | 251.10 | 248.70 |
| 3-09-77 | 236.50 | 248.30 | 243.20 |
| 3-10-77 | 242.70 | 257.00 | 253.20 |
| 3-11-77 | (230.50) | 236.00 | 242.80 |
| 3-17-77 | (246.50) | 236.40 | 252.80 |
| 3-18-77 | 236.60 | 224.50 | 241.80 |
| 3-21-77 | 243.50 | 250.30 | 254.50 |
| 3-23-77 | (236.00) | 242.70 | 236.10 |

* ( ) indicates intermediate terminus

Table 6A. Commodity Swing Prices July Soybean Meal.

## WHAT IS MARKET BALANCE AND HOW DOES IT WORK?

*Answer:*

The subject of market balance is the basis for considerable research. Within the Trident algorithm, balance is a function of repetition of the immediate past price action. The actual swing price $P_n$ is a balance price; i.e. the market was in balance when $P_n$ formed. Market balance is a compound concept because there must be a reference linking balance to what would otherwise constitute out-of-balance. In other words, "the market is in balance relative to what?"

Trident balance prices are reference prices which, when compared to the actual $P_n$, indicate the degree of out-of-balance (positive or negative) existing as of the current swing. Trident balance prices ($B_1, B_2, B_3, \ldots, B_n$) are unique theoretical price levels at which the market net variance is equal to zero. (Net variance equal to zero means that: $(P_1 - T_1,) + (P_2 - T_2) + (P_3 - T_3) + \ldots + (P_n - T_n) = 0$). The Trident target is, therefore, the reference price which defines balance. The relationship between $P_n$ and $T_n$ ($P_n - T_n$) will raise or lower the Trident balance prices so as to indicate overbought or oversold market conditions.

*Discussion:*

There is another kind of balance which is more significant from a forecasting mode that has not been discussed thus far. Consider the Trident:

$$P_1, P_2, P_3$$

at $P_1$, there was a target T, such that $(P_1 - T_1) = V_1$ (variance at $P_1$).

Likewise there was variance at $P_2$ ($P_2$ - $T_2$) and variance at $P_3$ ($P_3$ - $T_3$). Then the concept of total variance would be:

$$V_T = V_1 + V_2 + V_3$$

and, therefore, each Trident set can be thought of as having a total net variance ($V_T$).

Suppose the total net variance $V_T$ at $P_3$ was the same at $P_4$; i.e. the variance did not change. Then such a market could be thought of as being in balance relative to the total net variance contained within the Trident set. This means that there is a price level for each swing where the total net variance in the new Trident forming is equal to the total net variance within the previous Trident set. This idea is very different from the concept of zero balance but, from this idea, comes the basis for measuring price momentum in the market. The equation for the price level at which the variances are in balance is:

$$\boxed{\text{Bal. price} = P_3 + P_2 - T_1}$$

(derivation of this equation is omitted. However, it follows directly from substituting the difference between $P_1$ and $P_4$).

**Momentum**, simply stated, is the rate of change in balance during the last swing. Consider the swing $P_3$ to $P_4$; there was a calculated balance price at $P_3$ and $P_4$, such that ($P_3$ - Bp) = $F_3$ and ($P_4$ - $B_{P4}$) = $F_4$. The comparison between the balance factor at $P_3$ ($F_3$) and the balance factor at $P_4$ ($F_4$) namely:

$$(F_4 - F_3)$$

is the rate of change in balance during the last swing. Therefore:

$$\text{momentum} = (P_4 - B_{P4}) - (P_3 - B_{P3})$$

or,

$$\text{momentum} = (F_4 - F_3)$$

since the balance price uses T in the calculation, observe that a double Trident set (six prices) is needed in order to complete the calculation. In other words, $P_1$, $P_2$, $P_3$, $P_4$, $P_5$ and $P_6$ are required where $P_4$, $P_5$ and $P_6$ represent the current Trident set. Using this notation, the equation for momentum as of the last swing ($P_6$) is:

$$\boxed{M = P_6 + P_3 + T_3 - (2P_5 + T_2)}$$

Momentum is either positive, negative or zero. The general rule is:

AS MOMENTUM APPROACHES ZERO THE CLOSER IN BALANCE THE MARKET HAS BECOME.

The two concepts of market balance, zero balance and balance price, are not mutually exclusive. The difference between the three (3) swing balance prices and the three (3) swing zero balance prices is $V_T$ such that:

$$\boxed{B_3 + V_T = B_P}$$

Market balance is a consequence of the Trident algorithm $P_1 + P_4 = P_2 + P_3$. However, it is logical to assume that all unstable conditions seek to exist in balance. Commodity markets swing up and down in price, seeking to establish a balance between buyer and seller. Momentum measures the bias between bull and bear forces in the market, yet zero balance points to that theoretical calm price region where both bull and bear would be content (never happen).

## CAN TRIDENT STRATEGY BE USED FOR TRADE PYRAMIDING?

*Answer:*

Yes, Trident Strategy can be used for trade pyramiding. Pyramiding involves two (2) or more trades in the same direction with different entry prices, using profit gained from earlier trades to offset margin requirements in later trades. Trident pyramiding involves continuous trading in two (2) or more successive action swings such that all positions are offset at the same time.

There are substantial risks associated with pyramiding. In order to reduce these risks, it would be necessary to adopt a pyramiding strategy. This strategy would accomplish the following:

1. Limit the number of swings involved in the pyramid.
2. Establish pyramid qualifications tests.
3. Establish a basis for offsetting the pyramid.
4. Provide an adequate pyramid base.

*Discussion:*

Pyramiding can be successfully accomplished at several swing levels, namely, Intermediate swings and Minor swings. Intermediate swings occur along the path of Major action and Major reaction swings. Minor swings occur along the path of Intermediate action and Intermediate reaction swings. This is well established for all commodities. In most instances there are at least two (2) Intermediate action swings along the path of a Major swing. Likewise, there are at least two (2) Minor action swings along the path of an Intermediate swing. Considering this two (2) swing axiom, a Trident pyramid should not be attempted beyond (2) action swings (Intermediate or Minor).

In basic Trident Strategy, reaction swings are not traded. A Trident pyramid likewise should not be attempted along the path of the next higher level reaction swing. An Intermediate swing level pyramid stands a considerably better chance along the path of a Major action swing. Likewise, a Minor swing level pyramid stands a substantially better chance along the path of an Intermediate action swing. Therefore, the first pyramid qualification test is whether or not the pyramid is along the path of a higher level action swing.

The only reason a Trident pyramid will not succeed is if a trend reversal occurred after the first stage of the pyramid had been completed. In single trade Trident Strategy, changes in the relationship between B2 and B6 signal corresponding changes in trend direction. If there were a change in the relationship between B2 and B6 occurring just before or at the P3 base of the Trident pyramid, then there is a strong possibility that the pyramid would fail. Therefore, the second qualification test for a Trident pyramid is whether or not there was a change in the relationship between B2 and B6 occurring just before or at the base of the Trident pyramid.

Trident Trading Strategy provides several conditions under which a single trade should be offset. These rules continue to apply to a two (2) stage Trident pyramid. After the first level of trades is initiated, these trades must be managed in every way consistent with Trident Strategy. Once these trades have reached the window, or target, or beyond, any reaction swing that violates the trend reversal price (.625 retracement of the action swing) forces the pyramid base to be offset. If a subsequent reaction swing forms a new P3 within the P3 window, then the second level of the pyramid can be entered. Once the second level of the pyramid is established, then the entire pyramid should be managed as if all contracts in the pyramid were purchased (or sold) at the second entry level price.

A goal of pyramiding is to use profits accumulated from the base of the pyramid to offset margin requirements for positions at the top of the pyramid. This means that there should be more contracts at the base of the pyramid than at the top. Suppose three (3) contracts made up the base of a Trident pyramid and one (1) contract made up the second level (top). The profit accumulation from the first three (3) contracts would subsequently offset margin requirements for the fourth (4) contract. Therefore, a 3-1 structure would be ideal and it would follow that any multiple of 3-1 (6-2, 12-4, etc.) would likewise suffice.

Consider the Pork Belly price data (Table 7A). On 8/12 it is observed that the low 53.20 (8/9) was an intermediate terminus and the current low 55.90 could be a base for a Trident pyramid. Based upon this assumption, a trader would calculate the $B_2$, $B_6$ relationship (Table 8A) to determine if a trend change is forecast. It's observed that $B_2$ (55.54; 8/11) was below $B_6$ (59.62), and now for the current swing $B_2$ (52.00) is above $B_6$ (50.50). A trend change is indicated such that the next peak after the current swing would terminate an uptrend.

For purposes of discussion, what would happen if a Trident pyramid was attempted even though the $B_2$ - $B_6$ qualification test was not passed?

$P_1$ (53.20), $P_2$ (57.10), $P_3$ (55.90)

entry: 56.88

On 8/13, three (3) contracts would be bought at 56.90 showing a profit by the close (58.05) of $1242.00 that day. The next day the market reaches 58.50 and begins to retrace. Should the market retrace more than 62.5% of the action swing the pyramid must be offset.

| | | |
|---|---|---|
| TRP | = | .625 (55.90 - 58.50) + 58.50 |
| | = | 56.875 |

On 8/17, the market moves below 56.87 and the pyramid is offset. Oddly enough, the entry and the offset price are only 1 tick different!

On the same day (8/17), a new P3 low is formed (55.95) which appears to be an intermediate phantom low and, therefore, another Trident pyramid could be attempted.

P1 (55.90), P2 (58.50), P3 (55.95)

Entry: 56.60

On 8/17, three contracts are bought at 56.60. By 8/19, the market had risen to 59.80 ($3,456.00) and began to retrace to form a new P3 low. The P3 Window is calculated:

| | | |
|---|---|---|
| Determinate | = | .625 (55.90 - 57.15) + 59.80 |
| | = | 59.01 |
| TRP | = | .625 (55.95 - 59.80) + 59.80 |
| | = | 57.39 |

On 8/20, the market forms a new P3 (58.65) within the P3 Window and begins to move up again.

P1 (55.95), P2 (59.80), P3 (58.65)

Entry: 59.61 SD: - .287

On 8/20, a fourth contract is bought at 59.62 near the close. The pyramid is now complete. The market opens high the next trading session and moves up to 61.35 (8/23).

On 8/24, the market opens sharply lower and stops the trade out at 60.35 for a total profit of $4,312.80.

These examples of Trident pyramids indicate several important ideas:

(1) Pyramiding is not any more risky than Trident single swing trading.
(2) Pyramiding can be very profitable if done under the proper qualification tests.

The opportunity to pyramid will occur from time to time and represent significant trading possibilities.

Commodity: Pork Bellies May '77

| DATE | OPEN | HIGH | LOW | CLOSE |
|---|---|---|---|---|
| 7-20-76 | 57.70 | 58.60 | (57.70) | 58.60 |
| 7-21-76 | 59.50 | (60.60) | 59.50 | 60.55 |
| 7-22-76 | 60.10 | 60.65 | (59.30) | 60.60 |
| 7-23-76 | 60.50 | 62.60 | 60.50 | 62.60 |
| 7-26-76 | 62.85 | ((62.85)) | 60.60 | 60.60 |
| 7-27-76 | 59.50 | 59.60 | 58.60 | 58.60 |
| 7-28-76 | 56.60 | 58.50 | (56.60) | 58.15 |
| 7-29-76 | 57.60 | (59.20) | 57.30 | 58.80 |
| 7-30-76 | 57.90 | 59.15 | 57.40 | 57.55 |
| 8-02-76 | 56.80 | 56.80 | 55.55 | 55.55 |
| 8-03-76 | 54.50 | 55.80 | (54.40) | 54.75 |
| 8-04-76 | 55.20 | 55.75 | 54.45 | 55.70 |
| 8-05-76 | 56.25 | 57.35 | 56.25 | 56.92 |
| 8-06-76 | 57.37 | (57.37) | 54.92 | 55.00 |
| 8-09-76 | 55.30 | 55.50 | ((53.20)) | 53.35 |
| 8-10-76 | 53.40 | 55.35 | 53.30 | 55.35 |
| 8-11-76 | 56.40 | (57.15) | 55.90 | 56.65 |
| 8-12-76 | 56.10 | 56.85 | (55.90) | 56.05 |
| 8-13-76 | 56.70 | 58.05 | (56.35) | 58.05 |
| 8-16-76 | 58.40 | (58.50) | 57.25 | 57.95 |
| 8-17-76 | 57.45 | 57.45 | (55.95) | 57.05 |
| 8-18-76 | 57.50 | 59.05 | 57.45 | 59.05 |
| 8-19-76 | 58.90 | (59.80) | 58.50 | 58.75 |
| 8-20-76 | 59.00 | 59.75 | (58.65) | 59.62 |
| 8-23-76 | 60.50 | ((61.35)) | 60.30 | 61.30 |
| 8-24-76 | 60.35 | 60.35 | 59.50 | 59.60 |
| 8-25-76 | 59.60 | 59.60 | 57.70 | 58.17 |
| 8-26-76 | 58.60 | 59.00 | (56.80) | 57.10 |

Table 7A

Commodity: Pork Bellies May '77

| DATE | ACTUAL | $B_2$ | $B_6$ |
|---|---|---|---|
| 7-21-76 | 60.60 | | |
| 7-22-76 | 59.30 | | |
| 7-26-76 | 62.85 | 57.90 | 58.10 |
| 7-28-76 | 56.60 | 60.90 | 59.30 |
| 7-29-76 | 59.20 | 65.10 | 62.65 |
| 8-03-76 | 54.40 | 53.90 | 52.20 |
| 8-06-76 | 57.37 | 55.55 | 56.50 |
| 8-09-76 | 53.20 | 52.20 | 56.00 |
| 8-11-76 | 57.15 | 55.54 | 59.62 |
| 8-12-76 | 55.90 | 52.00 | 50.50 |
| 8-16-76 | 58.50 | 56.93 | 53.50 |
| 8-17-76 | 55.95 | 58.60 | 53.70 |
| 8-19-76 | 59.80 | 59.85 | 56.67 |
| 8-20-76 | 58.65 | 56.00 | 54.75 |
| 8-23-76 | 61.35 | 61.10 | 59.58 |

Table 8A. Pork Belly Swing Data

## WILL THERE BE ADDITIONAL TRIDENT DEVELOPMENTS?

*Answer:*

Yes, there will be periodic Trident developments. Research is continuing even as these additional pages are being written. Not only is active research being carried out here but many Trident students are actively trying out new ideas using basic Trident principles.

*Discussion:*

Trident holds the basic promise that an equation exists which properly understood and applied would predict with absolute accuracy every swing price before the swing occurs. The equation would contain certain elements which would fix a unique balance between what the market did in the most recent past and what the market must do in the immediate future. Such an equation is called a simulator with general form:

T = reference price + momentum + move + variance

where:

| | |
|---|---|
| **Reference price** | is a calculated price such as balance price or Zero balance price or perhaps actual P3. |
| **Momentum** | is the rate of change of balance in the market. |
| **Move** | is the last move completed or the previous move in the swing direction, or maybe some theoretical calculated move. |

**Variance** is some adjustment factor from the last actual result and the calculated target.

Equations of this form do yield interesting results. Particular simulators have generated exact prices for up to five (5) successive swings, only to break down for some unpredictable reason. Some simulators have been useful in predicting whether or not the Trident target will be reached or surpassed. One particular simulator has been very good at forecasting trend reversals. However, no simulator has been found that is completely reliable.

Studies are presently underway examining the balance configuration just before a major breakout. These studies are very fruitful so far and suggest that congestion (narrow trading range) with alternating intermediate swings leads to major moves or run away markets (point and figure chartists know this formation). Before the results of these studies can be incorporated into basic Trident Strategy, there will have to be many more tests and many more examples will have to be examined.

Different price phenomena have been observed and tentative classifications given. Such phenomena as echoes (repeating price pattern just before a major swing terminus) have been observed. Likewise, double phantom swings (swing within the high and low of the day) have been observed. Classifications such as platforms (double top) and bridges (double bottom) have been noted. Yet each kind of price action phenomena must remain the subject of future research and exploration.

Every Trident trader should view himself as a student of the market, because through additional study and observation discoveries will be made which will ultimately make money. Tubbs was quite correct over fifty years ago when he said "no problem in the market cannot be solved given sufficient thought and meditation."

# ADDENDUM

# TIME TRIALS

Time testing a new trading strategy is impossible without a certain amount of magic. A leap through time remains beyond current technology. "Time Trials" is a reflective discussion and update covering the question of validity and longevity of the Trident Strategy. Will the strategy hold up as a function of time?

The future for Commodity trading is one of continued growth. The Commodities Future Trading Commission (CFTC) has become fully operational; Compliance, Oversight, and Enforcement. Every Commodity Exchange has grown bigger and better mechanized. There are more commodity transactions than ever before. In spite of the growth in size and regulatory control, the mechanics of the real Commodity market have not changed. What was true continues to be true, without any significant changes planned for the foreseeable future.

Time Trials are based on various Trident trading scenarios moving forward in time by five year increments. Pork Bellies will be used for each test year (1980, 1985, 1990). Since research continues to reveal more and more about Trident and the market in general, new discoveries as a function of time will be included where applicable. New material will be presented, without rigor, as an integral part of Trident.

Ever wonder what happens to trading strategies during major financial disasters? How did Trident fare in the S&P 500 Futures before and during the Great 1987 Stock Market Crash? Can technical trading systems hold true during times of great economic upheaval and abruptly changing fundamentals? These questions will be answered in a special Time Trial covering October 1987.

Time Trials will use the same narrative format and style as the "TRIDENT CASE HISTORY;" including initial market analysis, calculations and broker orders. It is the process of analysis that's important. A profitworthy trade is the objective.

Trident Strategy was a major breakthrough in the mid '70s. Price swings were a new concept to most commodity traders. They are still new to many traders today. Few traders felt very comfortable with a purely mechanical trading system. The "Random Walk" theory was the ultimate argument against any technical system's claim to superiority. A common belief was that "Most systems worked some of the time, but sooner or later even the best technical system must fail!" Gurus would warn clients whenever their system was not working by saying, "I'll let you know when my system is working again."

Trident's approach was different. It used an algorithmic market model. The Trident algorithm was based on a presumed fluid balance between buying and selling pressure, with each taking alternate control of the market. The model predicted that "all buyers and sellers will meet ultimately in the middle." Furthermore, the market consisted of both active and inactive players where price was the sole discriminant. Even though a trader is not in the market (neither long or short), the "right" price will eventually force a market response.

Time trials will test the Trident algorithm, along with breakthroughs resulting from Trident research, in an attempt to validate its continuing relevancy.

PORK BELLIES FEB '81

**October 7, 1980** 64.85 66.50[1] 64.85[2] 65.10[1]
*early evening*

The following price data was obtained from Commodity Systems Inc. (CSI). However, any reliable data source would have done just as well:

| DATE | OPEN | HIGH | LOW | CLOSE | SEQ |
|---|---|---|---|---|---|
| 09/19/80 | 69.75 | 71.57 | 69.75 | 71.57 | 0 |
| 09/22/80 | 71.75 | ((72.10)) | 70.00 | 70.07 | 1 |
| 09/23/80 | 68.07 | 68.07 | 68.07 | 68.07 | 1 |
| 09/24/80 | 66.07 | 66.65 | 66.07 | 66.07 | 1 |
| 09/25/80 | 66.50 | (67.15) | (65.70) | 66.77 | 0 |
| 09/26/80 | 66.70 | 67.05 | 64.77 | 64.80 | 1 |
| 09/29/80 | 64.00 | 66.80 | ((63.50)) | 66.80 | 0 |
| 09/30/80 | 67.20 | ((67.80)) | 66.27 | 66.92 | 0 |
| 10/01/80 | 67.30 | 67.67 | 65.85 | 66.00 | 1 |
| 10/02/80 | 65.40 | 65.70 | 64.00 | 64.00 | 1 |
| 10/03/80 | 62.80 | 63.20 | ((62.02)) | 62.60 | 1 |
| 10/06/80 | 63.50 | 64.60 | 63.50 | 64.60 | 0 |
| 10/07/80 | 64.85 | 66.50 | 64.85 | 65.10 | 0 |

Each minor swing high and low are ringed and analyzed, looking for immediate highs and lows. Observe that the high low sequence (SEQ) has been added to the price analysis. The SEQ code is: 0 = low first, 1 = high first.

$I_1$ (63.50, $I_2$ (67.80), $I_3$ (62.02)

Intermediate Target (IT):

$$
\begin{aligned}
IT &= I_2 + I_3 - I_1 \\
&= 67.80 + 62.025 - 63.50 \\
&= 66.325
\end{aligned}
$$

The most current Minor trident is identified:

$P_1$ (63.50), $P_2$ (67.80), $P_3$ (62.02)

Minor Target (T):

$$
\begin{aligned}
T &= P_2 + P_3 - P_1 \\
&= 67.80 + 62.025 - 63.50 \\
&= 66.325
\end{aligned}
$$

*(In this case Minor Trident and Intermediate Trident are the same.) Minor target has been reached and exceeded (66.50).* The short term (B2) and long term (B6) are calculated:

*current* $B_2 = 2(P_2) - P0$
$= 2(67.80) - 67.15$
$= 68.45$

*current* $B_6 = P_2 + P_{-2} - P_{-4}$
$= 67.80 + 72.10 - 71.30$
$= 68.60$

*The market is below both the long and short balance prices. Observe $B_6$ above $B_2$.*

$$\text{next swing} \quad B_2 = 2(P_3) - P_1 = 2(62.025) - 63.50 = 60.55$$

$$\text{next swing} \quad B_6 = P_3 + P_{-1} - P_{-3} = 62.025 + 66.075 - 68.55 = 59.55$$

*$B_6$ moves below $B_2$, which signals a Trend reversal. This market should be bought upon the next low!*

Calculate a $P_3$ window:

$$\text{Determinate (D)} = .625\,(P_2 - P1) + P_3 = .625\,(67.80 - 63.50) + 62.025 = \underline{64.7125}$$

$$\text{Trend Reversal (TR)} = .625\,(P_2 - P_3) + P_3 = .625\,(67.80 - 62.025) + 62.025 = \underline{65.6343}$$

Today's high (66.50) is beyond the "selling" window (65.65) which supports the $B_2$, $B_6$ Trend Reversal idea. Another $P_3$ window can be calculated that could support a trade to the upside. If $I_3$ is 62.025, then both current and previous minor swings are action swings. In fact, the last four minor swings are action swings. The last reaction swing was 66.075 - 67.15, which occurred 9/24/80 - 9/25/80.

Calculate a $P_3$ window for the next trade to the upside:

$$\text{Determinate (D)} = .625\,(P_{-1} - P_0) + P_3$$
$$= .625\,(66.075 - 67.15) + 66.50$$
$$= \underline{65.828}$$

$$\text{Trend Reversal (TR)} = .625\,(P_2 - P_3) + P_3$$
$$= .625\,(62.025 - 66.50) + 66.50$$
$$= \underline{63.70}$$

Calculate Entry Differential (ED):

$$\text{Entry Differential} = (P3 - P2)/4$$
$$= (66.50 - 62.025)/4$$
$$= 1.11875$$

| Intermediate Trident | | | IT | Minor Trident | | | $B_2$ | $B_6$ | $P_3$ Window | Entry Diff |
|---|---|---|---|---|---|---|---|---|---|---|
| $I_1$ | $I_2$ | $I_3$ | | $P_1$ | $P_2$ | $P_3$ | 68.45 | 68.60 | | |
| 63.50 | 67.80 | 62.02 | 66.325 | 67.80 | 62.02 | 66.50 | 60.55 | 59.55 | 65.825 - 63.70 | 1.11875 |

**October 8, 1980** 65.00 66.95[2] 64.40[1] 66.02 0
*early evening*

A Broker instruction is given:

***BUY A FEB '81 BELLY UPON ANY RALLY OF 1.125 FROM THE LOWEST PRICE REACHED. CANCEL ORDER IF MARKET MOVES BELOW 63.70.***

*The market opened at 65.00 and continued down to 64.40. A rally ensued which triggered a "Buy" at 65.525.*

Based on conversation with a Broker, the following Information Line can be calculated:

| Trident Prices | | | Target | Critical | Entry | Profit | Stop | Stop | Risk |
|---|---|---|---|---|---|---|---|---|---|
| P1 | P2 | P3 | Price | Price | Price | Amount | Protected | Differential | Amount |
| 62.02 | 66.50 | 64.40 | 68.875 | 66.6375 | 65.525 | $1,206.00 | 64.375 | -.525 | $414.00 |

A specific Broker order is given:

***BUY A FEB '81 BELLY 65.52***
***OBJECTIVE 68.87***
***PROTECTIVE STOP 64.375***

*The trade was executed at the entry price and went on to close at 66.82 ($468.00).*
Observe the minor target (68.875) is in conflict with the intermediate target (66.325). But the intermediate is also a minor target, since both minor and intermediate prices were the same. This conflict can be resolved easily by looking at the major target ($M_1$ (57.60), $M_2$ (72.10), $M_3$ (62.02)) or

$$\text{Major (T)} = 62.025 + 72.10 - 57.60 = 76.525$$

**October 9, 1980** 66.60 68.82$^2$ 66.50$^1$ 68.82 0
*evening*

The minor target was almost reached. However, price limit restraints prevailed (200 points). The market has confirmed each assumption and appears to want to go higher.

*By now, specific research started in "Market Math" had created a new discipline called "Factor Analysis." Its function is to predict the next "High" and "Low" as entry and objective for a Day Trade. Factor Analysis is a systematic method for analyzing factors which effect future price. Suppose there were more profit in a trade than the minor target indicated. Factor Analysis could be used to discover this.*

*The calculation is as follows:*

$$P_1 = S_a + C - S_1 + (H_p - H) + (S_a - L) + [(I_2 - H) + (S_1 - I_3)]$$
$$= 66.6125 + 68.825 - 64.40 + 66.95 - 68.825 + 66.6125 - 66.50 + 67.80 - 68.825 + 64.40 - 62.025$$
$$= 70.625$$

$$P_2 = P_1 + S_a - H$$
$$= 70.625 + 66.6125 - 68.825$$
$$= 68.4125$$

*Based on these calculations this market should continue to go up well beyond the minor Trident target! In practice, the Factor Analysis calculations would be made each day, looking for an optimum target. If the next Factor Analysis objective were used as an adjusted target the trade profit would be $1,836.00 or $630.00 better! Factor Analysis is a very powerful tool. However, the stop differential is powerful as well. If the SD = .525 were used to offset this trade there is:*

*71.80 - .525 = 71.275 or $234.00 more profit.*

*If it is desireable to let the profits run, consider using the SD as an anytime trade exit whenever $P_1$ equals $I_3$.*

**October 10, 1980** 69.20 $70.25^2$ $68.40^1$ 69.80 0
*morning*

The market opened (69.20) beyond the minor target. Based on an order to sell (68.875), the trade would make about $1,323.00. If no sell order was given the SD could be used to offset the trade (69.20 - .525 = 68.675) resulting in less profit ($72) then the original objective. However, $1,323.00 is a good profit considering the amount of effort expended.

A FEW YEARS LATER . . .

*Let's move ahead a few years to 1985. Factor Analysis research led to a refined reliable technology. No new trades are made without calculating Factor Analysis. The goal is a maximized Trade Entry within a few ticks of the ring (P3). Price data is processed with more detail; noting sequence, gaps, compound swings, as well as minor, intermediate, and major rings. It's significant whether a market opens gap-up or gap-down.*

*May '85 Bellies will be the subject of another Time Trial. It could have been any actively traded market for purposes of this discussion. However, it is well known and proven in countless calculations . . . ALL COMMODITY MARKETS ARE THE SAME! All markets use the same mechanics, the same equations, rules and procedures within the same configuration. The Trident algorithm does not change because the name of the commodity changes. Another more interesting aspect of commodity price action is the manner in which "tomorrow's prices are fixed and locked in by today's results."*

PORK BELLIES MAY '85

**February 4, 1985** 74.58 74.90[1] 72.55[2] 72.75[1] 1
*late night*

The following data was obtained from Commodity Systems, Inc. However, any reliable data source would have sufficed.

| DATE | OPEN | HIGH | LOW | CLOSE | SEQ |
|---|---|---|---|---|---|
| 01/24/85 | 72.50 | (74.05) | 72.10 | 73.37 | 0 |
| 01/25/85 | 73.37 | 73.70 | (72.75) | 73.10 | 1 |
| 01/28/85 | 74.50 | (75.00) | 73.35 | 74.35 | 0 |
| 01/29/85 | 74.25 | 74.80 | 74.05 | 74.30 | 1 |
| 01/30/85 | 74.10 | 74.80 | (73.52) | 74.67 | 0 |
| 01/31/85 | 75.00 | ((75.15)) | 72.70 | 72.75 | 1 |
| 02/01/85 | 72.58 | 74.60 | 72.40 | 74.50 | 0 |
| 02/04/85 | 74.58 | 74.90 | 72.55 | 72.75 | 1 |

$I_1$ (78.20), $I_2$ (70.75), $I_3$ (75.15)

Intermediate Target (IT):

$$\begin{aligned} IT &= I_2 + I_3 - I_1 \\ &= 70.75 + 75.15 - 78.20 \\ &= 67.70 \end{aligned}$$

The most current Minor trident:

$$P_1\ (75.15),\ P_2\ (72.40),\ P_3\ (74.90)$$

has a Minor target (T) 72.15. Since the Intermediate target is down, and has a long way to go, trades to the downside should have a better chance for success. Consider today's low as an assumptive P3 . . . then:

$$P_1\ (72.40),\ P_2\ (74.90),\ P_3\ (72.55)$$

would be the basis for a downside entry window. Observe both minor swings (P1 to P2) and (P2 to P3) are action swings with a new I3 (P1 72.40). If the market does not move higher the next I3 would be (P2 74.90). The problem this presents is resolved by finding the last minor reaction swing, which in this instance is (73.52 to 75.15). Therefore:

Determinate (D) = .625 (75.15 - 73.525) + 72.55
= 73.565

Trend Reversal (TR) = .625 (74.90 - 72.55) + 72.55
= 74.025 *rounded to nearest tick*

The short term ($B_2$) and long term ($B_6$) are as follows:

*current* $B_2 = 2(P_2) - P_0$
$= 2(74.90) - 75.15$
$= 74.65$

*current* $B6 = P2 + P_{-2} - P_{-4}$
$= 74.90 + 75.00 - 74.05$
$= 75.85$

*The market is below both long and short term balance prices.*

*current swing* $B2 = 2(P3) - P1$
$= 2(72.55) - 72.40$
$= 72.70$

*current swing* $B6 = P3 + P_{-1} - P_{-3}$
$= 72.55 + 73.525 - 72.75$
$= 73.325$

*The relationship between B2 and B6 does not change during the next two swings. Therefore, the assumption that the intermediate trend will continue downward is reasonable.*

**February 5, 1985** 72.83 73.90[2] 72.60[1] 73.82[5] 0
*later that day*

The market moved into the P3 window (73.565 - 74.025) and has closed three (3) ticks off the high.

| Intermediate Trident | | | IT | Minor Trident | | | B2 | B6 | P3 Window | Entry Diff |
|---|---|---|---|---|---|---|---|---|---|---|
| $I_1$ | $I_2$ | $I_3$ | | $P_1$ | $P_2$ | $P_3$ | 74.65 | 75.85 | | |
| 78.20 | 70.75 | 75.15 | 67.70 | 72.40 | 74.90 | 72.55 | 72.70 | 73.325 | 73.565 - 74.025 | -.5875 |

It is clear that should this market move up more than a few ticks the Trend Reversal (TR) (74.025) will be penetrated. If the market fails to move higher, then a trade to the downside will be triggered.

| Trident Prices | | | Target | Critical | Entry | Profit | Stop | Stop | Risk |
|---|---|---|---|---|---|---|---|---|---|
| P1 | P2 | P3 | Price | Price | Price | Amount | Protected | Differential | Amount |
| 74.90 | 72.55 | 73.90 | 71.55 | 72.725 | 73.30 | $630.00 | 73.925 | .3375 | $225.00 |

*What will this market do tomorrow? This is precisely what "Factor Analysis" was designed to do. The first calculation $P_1$ determines the minor swing extension. $P_1$ predicts continued swing progress or minor swing termination by way of reversal. P2 calculates the opposite price pair (Stasis), which counterbalances the projected swing extension or reversal. Needless to say, Factor Analysis is the most powerful mechanical tool for single day forecasting ever developed. Factor Analysis involves quite a bit of accurate number crunching and for that reason, it is best handled by personal computer. There are at least 480 different combinations of factors, conditions, and considerations defined by current market action. Factor Analysis calculations will be included in these "Time Trials" as a matter of interest. However, this book is not the proper forum for teaching Factor Analysis other than a few broad concepts. With this in mind, the equations yield the following results:*

$$
\begin{aligned}
P_1 &= S_a + C - S_1 + [(L - P_1) + (H - S_a)] + (S_a - L_p) + (C - H)] \\
&= 73.775 + 73.825 - 75.15 + [(72.60 - 72.40) + (73.90 - 75.15)] \\
&\quad + (73.775 - 74.90) + 73.825 - 73.90) \\
&= 70.20
\end{aligned}
$$

$$
\begin{aligned}
P_2 &= P_1 + S_a - S_2 + (S_1 - C) + (H - C) \\
&= 70.20 + 73.775 - 72.40 + (75.15 - 73.825) + (73.90 - 73.825) \\
&= 72.975
\end{aligned}
$$

*The difference between P1 and P2 represents nearly $1000.00 ($999)! That's an amount worthy of whatever reason people trade commodities. But observe that according to this calculation the Trident Entry (73.30) will be skipped over basis the P2 high (72.975). BUT! You trade commodities to make money. RIGHT! Should this trade be made? Fortunately, this is not the question. The question is what is the best way to make this trade within a Trident discussion. Notice, there would be no question if Factor Analysis were being traded.*

7 a.m. a broker instruction is given:

> ***SELL MAY BELLY 73.30 STOP***
> ***CANCEL TRADE IF BELLIES***
> ***MOVE ABOVE 74.02.***

**February 6, 1985** 72.84 72.97[1] 71.82[2] 71.82 1

*The market opens within a range (72.85) which triggers the Stop Order. Factor Analysis proved to be right on track. Observe the target (71.55) is below limit down. Since this trade will continue for at least one more day, and given the indication that this market may exceed the target, some consideration should be given to trade Offset. Original Trident calls for offset at the target without equivocation. The SD (.3375) could be used. Or, what about using the swing extension $P_1$ (70.20)! Well, the market needs a little bit of room (6 ticks), say 70.35. Actually, it would be better to use the TOOL . . . Factor Analysis. And that's exactly what ought to be done at this point because that's what it was designed to do. But, the calculation was already made and the swing extension $P_1$ (70.20) has not been reached. Right! Therefore, let the market* *confirm that it is still trying to reach $P_1$. The calculation is as follows:*

$$P_1 = S_a + C - S_1 + (S_2 - L) + S_a - H_p) + (0 - H) + C - L)$$
$$= 72.8625 + 71.825 - 73.90 + (72.40 - 71.825) + (72.8625 - 73.90) + (72.85 - 72.975) + 0$$
$$= 70.20$$

*Is it surprising that the market is still trying to do what it set out to do? Given this new information, the trade offset should be placed at 70.35 (or lower if you and your broker can handle it).*

**February 7, 1985** 71.05 71.50[1] 70.20[2] 70.47 1

S&P 500 INDEX MAR '88

| DATE | OPEN | HIGH | LOW | CLOSE | SEQ |
|---|---|---|---|---|---|
| 09/18/87 | 322.80 | 323.10 | 319.90 | 321.45 | 1 |
| 09/21/87 | 322.50 | (324.25) | 315.40 | 315.30 | 1 |
| 09/22/87 | 316.00 | 327.40 | ((314.70)) | 327.20 | 0 |
| 09/23/87 | 326.80 | (328.70) | 325.10 | 328.10 | 0 |
| 09/24/87 | 326.80 | 328.00 | 324.70 | 325.65 | 1 |
| 09/25/87 | 326.10 | 327.65 | (324.20) | 327.65 | 0 |
| 09/28/87 | 329.50 | 332.50 | 328.20 | 329.75 | 0 |
| 09/29/87 | 329.50 | (332.70) | 326.40 | 328.10 | 1 |
| 09/30/87 | 327.70 | 329.55 | (326.20) | 329.20 | 0 |
| 10/01/87 | 330.15 | 335.20 | 329.50 | 335.15 | 0 |
| 10/02/87 | 334.70 | ((336.60)) | 333.80 | 335.00 | 0 |

**October 2, 1987** 334.70 336.60[1] 333.80[2] 335.00 0
*Anytime after the close*

*One of the most important events that took place during the time frame of this discussion was the 1987 Stock Market Crash. The 1987 Crash started as an erosion on Friday, October 2, 1987. The high (336.60) ultimately became a Master High which lasted for several years. A Trident trader looking for the next trade to the upside (P1 332.50, P2 326.20, P3 336.60) would have observed the market pass quickly through the P3 window (332.65 - 330.10), signaling a possible trend reversal for trades to the upside. Billions of dollars were lost . . . not to mention careers, prestige and brokerage houses down the drain. But what happened to Trident Strategy? Did it hold up? Could it have produced perhaps one of the greatest trades of all time? Or did Trident go the way of everything else. The answers to these questions seem to be the key Time Trial, because if a trading strategy can't make it when everything is at stake, then how effective can it be when nothing is at stake?*

**October 5, 1987** 334.80 335.40[1] 331.90[2] 334.40 1
*Sometime after the close*

$P_1$ (332.50), $P_2$ (326.20), $P_3$ (336.60)

A look at balance prices reveals a trend change in process:

| | $B_2$ | $B_6$ |
|---|---|---|
| current | 328.20 | 323.10 |
| next | 340.70 | 341.05 |

Applying the trend change rules to the B2 B6 change:

"the next valley after the current swing will terminate a downtrend"

This means the market will move down to form a valley (ring), move up to form a peak (ring), move down to form a lower valley and reverse back to the upside. Based on this analysis it is clear that the market should be traded from the downside.

**October 6, 1987** 332.40 $333.20^{1}$ $323.30^{2}$ 323.40 1
*Midnight*

The P3 window begins 3.9375 from the lowest price reached. (3.9375 + 323.30 = 327.25). Should the market move up 3.9375, a new downside trade can be considered. The Entry differential is (326.20 - 336.60) /4 = -2.6. The trend change rule proved true, and current P3 (336.60) can be ringed as an Intermediate high. The current swing is the first swing in a new direction.

**October 7, 1987** 323.00 $325.60^{2}$ $321.20^{1}$ 324.20 0
*Bingo*

A rally ensued today. Mild compared to the recent slide but sufficient to cause the market to enter the P3 window: (321.20 + 3.9375 = 325.15). Should the market move down -2.60 from the high before moving through the window a new trade will trigger, i.e. Entry = 325.60 - 2.60 or 323.00 provided the market does not move higher tomorrow.

Factor Analysis should help answer any questions about tomorrow. The calculations are as follows:

$$P_1 = S_a + C - S_1 + (L_p - L) + (S_a - L_p) + (H - S_a) + (0 - L_p) + (H - C)$$
$$= 328.90 + 324.20 - 336.60 + (323.30 - 321.20) + 328.90 - 333.20)$$
$$+ (325.60 - 328.9) + 323 - 323.30) + (325.60 - 324.20)$$
$$= 312.10$$

$$P_2 = P_1 + S_a - (L + (S_a - C) + (L - O)$$
$$= 312.10 + 328.90 - 321.20 + (328.90 - 324.20) + (323.30 - 323.00)$$
$$= 324.80$$

Factor Analysis reveals a good trade to the downside ready to start tomorrow. The trade appears to take the market down toward the Trident target (310.20) but not reaching it. With a relatively short (1.11) stop differential ready to terminate the trade prematurely, it would be wiser to use the FA objective rather than the P2 window in tandem with the SD. By now, Factor Analysis is an old friend, something that has become comfortable to use and at the same time quite dependable. As a matter of fact, Factor Analysis P2 (324.80 less 6 ticks or 324.50) would be Entry for the downside trade. Making money is the primary reason for trading commodities. Go with what works. In other words, if a better trade comes along, take it!

**October 8, 1987** 324.60 324.75[1] 317.30[2] 319.45 1
*Shortly after the market opens*

> ***SELL A MAR '88 S&P 500 INDEX***
> ***323.00 STOP. CANCEL ORDER IF MARKET TRADES ABOVE 327.70***

| Trident Prices | | | Target | Critical | Entry | Profit | Stop | Stop | Risk |
|---|---|---|---|---|---|---|---|---|---|
| P1 | P2 | P3 | Price | Price | Price | Amount | Protected | Differential | Amount |
| 336.60 | 321.20 | 325.60 | 310.20 | 317.90 | 323.00 | $6,400.00 | 325.65 | 1.10 | $1,325 |

An easy decision is made to use the Factor Analysis Target (312.10 + .30 = 312.40) for trade offset ($5,300.00):

***BUY A MAR '88 S&P 500 INDEX 312.40. SELL A MAR '88 S&P 500 INDEX 325.65 STOP.***

In an actual trading situation trade Entry would be (324.80 - .30 = 324.50). The reason for this is twofold: (1) make more money; and (2) reduce the risk. The profit objective for this trade is $6,050.00, or $750.00 more, while risk is (324.80 + .30 = 325.10) $300.00, or $1,025.00 less. What's more practical than that!

**October 9, 1987** 319.00 320.70[1] 314.90[2] 315.80 1
*Evening*

The trade goes well. $4,350.00! So far so good.

Some thought should be given to the next P3 window because, according to the trend change rule, the downtrend has another leg to complete. The P3 window is:

Determinate (D) = .625 (332.50 - 326.20) + 312.10
= 316.05

Trend Reversal (TR) = .625 (336.60 - 312.10) + 312.10
= 327.40

The Target (312.10) is used as the tentative P3. An Entry Differential based on the current trade is:

Entry Differential (ED) = (312.10 - 325.60) /4
= -3.375

**October 12, 1987** 314.67 317.30[2] 312.00[1] 315.80 1
*Early session*

The target is reached with four (4) ticks to spare. Great! A minor adjustment to the $P_3$ window is made: (-.1 and -.375)

(D) = 315.95; (TR) - 327.3625

Will the next short trade trigger tomorrow? Factor Analysis calculations are as follows:

$$P_1 = S_a + C - S_1 + (P_f) + (S_f) + (G_f) + CS_f) + (N_f) + (C_f)$$

(General Form)

where: $P_f$ = Progress factor; $S_f$ = Swing factor
$G_f$ = Gap factor; $CS_f$ = Compound swing factor
$N_f$ = Nest factor; and $C_f$ = Close factor

$P_1$ = 324.3 + 315.10 - 336.60 + (314.90 - 312) + (324.30 - 317.30) - 312.00)
= 315.80

$$P_2 = P_1 + S_a - S_2 + (S_f) + (P_{1f}) \text{ (General Form)}$$

$P_2$ = 315.80 + 324.30 - 312.00 + (317.30 - 324.3) + (315.10 - 315.80)
= 320.40

*The general form of the Factor Analysis P1 and P2 have been included for your interest only. It should be observed that P1 is more complex than P2. In other words, if you know where the market is going then it's a simpler matter to know where you'd have to start. Keep in mind, however, that there are many different combinations of factors and events that determine the outcome.*

According to market analysis, this market should rally tomorrow. The rally appears to take the market deeper into the P3 window. ($2,300.00 on the day should not be ignored).

**October 13, 1987** 318.00 320.55[2] 315.90[1] 319.25 0
*Afterwards*

So far the market has yielded about $8,350.00 over the past eight (8) days ($1,043.75/day). ED for a new trade is -3.40 or 320.55 - 3.4 = 317.15. Will tomorrow's low trigger a new trade or will the rally continue or both . . .?

$$P_1 = S_a + C - S_1 + (H - S_2) + (S_a - H_p) + (S_1' - S_1) + (H - S_a) + (0 - H_p)$$
$$=- 318.8 + 319.25 - 325.60 + (320.55 - 312) + (318.8 - 317.3) + (325.6 - 336.6) + (320.55 - 324.3) + (318 - 317.30)$$
$$= 308.45$$

$$P_2 = P_1 + S_a - S_2 + (H_p - 0) + [(H_p - S_a) + S_a - H)]$$
$$= 308.45 + 318.8 - 312 + (317.30 - 318) + [(317.3 - 318.8) + (324.3 - 320.55)]$$
$$= 316.80$$

The S&P 500 Index Mar '88 might get pounded tomorrow! The Trident trade entry at 317.15 may be missed entirely. The best entry appears to be 316.8 - .30 = 316.50 or better.

| Trident Prices | | | Target | Critical | Entry | Profit | Stop | Stop | Risk |
|---|---|---|---|---|---|---|---|---|---|
| P1 | P2 | P3 | Price | Price | Price | Amount | Protected | Differential | Amount |
| 336.60 | 312.00 | 320.55 | 295.95 | 308.25 | 317.15 | $10,600 | 320.60 | 2.1375 | $1,725 |

Big profits generate big risks! Everything is relative, or is it? the true risk in this trade is Entry - Stop or 316.50 - 317.10 = .6 ($300.00). Sometime before the market opens:

***SELL A MAR '88 S&P 500 INDEX 316.50 OR BETTER. BUY A MAR '81 S&P 500 INDEX 317.10 STOP. UH! . . . UH! . . . MAKE THAT 317.50***

**October 14, 1987** 315.90 317.00[1] 308.55[2] 308.65 1
*1:30 PM PST*

That was scary! A tight Stop makes a very visible target. There is serious talk of a possible market collapse. It couldn't hurt! Today's action added $3,925.00 to the pot.

$$P_1 = S_a + C - S_1 + (P_2 - L) + (S_a - H) + (S_1 - CS_a)$$
$$=- 314.55 + 308.65 - 320.55 + (312 - 308.55) + (314.55 - 317) + (320.55 - 322.575)$$
$$= 301.625$$

$$P_2 = P_1 + S_a - S_2 + (CS_a - H) + (S_1 - P_1) + [(G_f)]$$
$$= 301.625 + 322.575 - 308.55 + (322.575 - 320.55) + (320.55 - 325.60) + [(317 - 319.25) + (317 - 315.90)]$$
$$= 311.475$$

Based on Factor Analysis calculations, tomorrow's move could be quite dramatic. In fact, the profit potential represented by the high-low range should not be overlooked. ($4,550.00)

***SELL A MAR '88 S&P 500 INDEX 311.10. BUY A MAR '88 S&P 500 INDEX 302. BUY A MAR '88 S&P 500 INDEX 312 STOP.***

**October 15, 1987** 306.15 311.30[1] 301.50[2] 301.80 1
*Just after the close*

Talk about a major stock market failure echoed throughout the market today. Gurus of gloom and doom are building larger audiences from anybody who will listen. Some of them don't mince words, they simply say "it's over!" Meantime, chalk up another $4,550.00.

The Trident target (295.95) has not been reached. The trade is ongoing. Will the market reach and exceed this target? Is there another trade available tomorrow?

$$P_1 = S_a + C - S_1 + (P_f) + (S_f) + (S_f) + (CS_f)$$
$$=- 311.025 + 301.8 - 320.55 + (308.55 - 301.5) + (311.025 - 311.3) + (306.15 - 308.55) + (320.55 - 336.60)$$
$$= 280.60$$

$$P_2 = P_1 + CS_a - S_2 + (CS_a - H) + (CS_a - S_1)$$
$$= 280.60 + 319.05 - 301.5 + (319.05 - 311.3) + 319.05 - 320.55)$$
$$= 304.40$$

The gloom boys were right. It is over! The only thing to do is follow this thing down as long as the numbers confirm more downside action. Yes! That's the only thing to do:

***SELL A MAR '88 S&P 500 INDEX 304. BUY A MAR '88 S&P 500 INDEX 281. BUY A MAR '88 S&P 500 INDEX 305 STOP.***

**October 16, 1987** 303.90 304.55[1] 280.40[2] 285.45 1

*At market's end*

Rake in another $11,500.00. There's no end in sight according to those who know these things. The market is starting to make seriously dangerous noise. Dangerous in the sense that panic is dangerous. Banks have started calling in loans; the market is one big margin call. They're threatening to raise S&P margins to chase the little people out. But what to worry, this market has contributed nearly $40,000.00 to a very worthy cause.

*later that night . . .*

$$P_1 = S_a + C - S_1 + (L_p - L) + (S_a - H) + [(CS_f)]$$
$$=- 300.475 + 285.45 - 320.55 + (301.50 - 280.4) + (300.475 - 304.55)$$
$$+ [(320.55 - 336.60) + (308.5 - 320.55)$$
$$= 254.30$$

$$P_2 = P_1 + S_a - S_2 + (CS_a - S_1) + (CS_a - H)$$
$$= 254.3 + 308.5 - 280.4 + (308.5 - 320.55) + (308.5 - 304.55)$$
$$= 274.30$$

A gap down high is expected tomorrow. However, the pattern does not appear to change. In fact, it's getting worse. The gap could be an exhaustion gap signaling the end of the down move.

***SELL A MAR '88 S&P 500 INDEX 273.70 STOP. BUY 2 MAR '88 S&P 500 INDEX 255. BUY 2 MAR '88 S&P 500 INDEX 274.80 STOP.***

## *BLACK MONDAY*

**October 19, 1987** 274.00 274.00[1] 200.00[2] 204.10 1
*Shortly after the open*

RING! . . . RING! . . . HELLO . . . YEAH! BE ADVISED THAT THE MARGIN FOR S&P 500 INDEX HAS BEEN RAISED TO $65,000.00. HOW DO YOU WANT TO HANDLE IT? . . . LIQUIDATE! . . . UH! . . . LIQUIDATE! WHERE IS IT NOW? 247? . . . 246? . . 241? IT'S OKAY, THE TRADE OBJECTIVE HAS BEEN REACHED!

All in all, the S&P 500 market represented a profit of $64,500.00 from a combination of Trident and Factor Analysis Day trades. There was more money to be made during the great '87 Stock Market Crash, but not so much for the general public. It took a long time before this market returned to normal.

Trident traders who traded S&P 500 during the Great Crash fared well. The system did not let them down. Those traders who knew Factor Analysis fared even better. It is significant that the B2 B6 trend change rules worked as predicted. The trend change rules were instrumental in signaling the downside opportunity exactly as described in this book ten (10) years earlier! At the very least, Trident strategy continues to make money and continues to hold true.

## THE NEXT DECADE

Trident Strategy has given way to much that flowed from it. Ring highs and lows are common to all systems that originated from Trident. Breakthrough after breakthrough have pushed market analysis beyond anything anybody ever thought possible.

RETROSTASIS is a new word that stands for the mechanics regulating commodity price action in an open outcry market. RETRO means back or backward, retard, inverse or reverse. STASIS means stoppage. Retrostasis as a concept implies some kind of reversing action. The commodity market creates price change as a means of balance between buyer and seller within a retrostatic transaction where buyer and seller transfer title at different prices. Retrostasis would not exist if both buyer and seller transferred title at the same price. If all the available supply at a given price was acquired, then price would have to rise or fall in order to balance supply. Any good book on Economics will define this process. The price movement on the day is balanced at the close (Settlement). The High and Low define the out-of-balance extremes. The next Open creates a starting balance, offsetting the retrostasis of the previous session. Through Retrostasis, the balances and extremes, *Open, High, Low and Close* can be calculated.

FEB '91 PORK BELLIES will be used to show new approaches to technical analysis. The Pork Belly market was selected for this discussion solely because of its universal appeal. (Bellies consistently outperform every other market when the criteria is profit vs. margin.) What works on Bellies works also on all other commodity markets.

Trident Strategy sought to trade about 50% of a Minor Action swing. It declared reaction swings persona non grata and warned against trade attempts. The strategy ruled out trading beyond the target. It screened trades which were in conflict with intermediate targets.

The safeguards deliberately placed in Trident Strategy became limiting and inefficient compared to the flexibility of Factor Analysis. Through Factor Analysis it was possible to make more from day trading than from trading the entire swing! Sometimes twice as much! It was inevitable that an interim system would be developed that combined Trident Strategy with Factor Analysis. It was dubbed *Swing Analysis.*

*Swing Analysis* is a logical consequence of Trident theory. Its objective is to trade 100% of a minor swing. *Swing Analysis* makes no distinction between action or reaction swing status. It was designed to calculate minor price swing targets in advance of their occurrence.

*Swing Analysis* is a classic example of applied Price Action mechanics. It achieves accuracy within a few ticks while keeping its user one or two swings ahead of the market! It is also the first *designer* system to combine two independent trading methods. The resultant *Swing Analysis* system allows its user to "position trade" similar to Trident with the precision of Factor Analysis.

*Swing Analysis* uses a ten (10) ring average ($R_a$) which is similar to the $S_a$ in Factor Analysis. The $R_a$ tends to define HIGH and LOW within the expression: BUY HIGH, SELL LOW. It's possible to make money by simply executing trades at the $R_a$. In theory, the $R_a$ is a long term price balance representing the price at roughly the average Open Interest.

PORK BELLIES FEB. '91

| DATE | OPEN | HIGH | LOW | CLOSE | SEQ |
|---|---|---|---|---|---|
| 07/03/90 | 56.10 | 56.10 | 54.05 | 54.85 | 1 |
| 07/05/90 | 55.05 | (56.45) | (54.00) | 55.42 | 0 |
| 07/06/90 | 55.45 | 56.25 | 54.60 | 55.85 | 0 |
| 07/09/90 | 55.20 | 55.80 | 54.50 | 54.90 | 1 |
| 07/10/90 | 55.00 | 55.85 | (54.20) | 55.52 | 0 |
| 07/11/90 | 55.00 | (55.90) | 54.50 | 54.57 | 1 |
| 07/12/90 | 55.00 | 55.30 | 52.95 | 53.22 | 1 |
| 07/13/90 | 53.40 | 54.50 | (52.50) | 54.12 | 0 |
| 07/16/90 | 54.40 | 55.30 | 53.60 | 54.92 | 0 |
| 07/17/90 | 55.25 | 56.92 | 55.25 | 56.20 | 0 |
| 07/18/90 | 56.60 | ((57.00)) | 54.60 | 54.80 | 1 |
| 07/19/90 | 53.80 | 54.40 | 52.80 | 52.80 | 1 |
| 07/20/90 | 52.00 | 53.85 | 51.80 | 51.90 | 1 |
| 07/23/90 | 51.60 | 51.75 | 49.90 | 49.90 | 1 |
| 07/24/90 | 49.60 | 51.90 | ((49.40)) | 51.90 | 0 |
| 07/25/90 | 53.90 | 53.90 | 53.90 | 53.90 | 0 |
| 07/26/90 | 55.70 | (55.70) | 53.75 | 54.35 | 1 |
| 07/27/90 | 54.30 | 54.55 | (53.45) | 54.07 | 1 |
| 07/30/90 | 54.30 | 56.05 | 54.15 | 55.72 | 0 |
| 07/31/90 | 56.50 | 57.72 | 56.20 | 57.72 | 0 |
| 08/01/90 | 58.60 | ((59.12)) | 55.72 | 55.72 | 1 |
| 08/02/90 | 54.20 | 54.25 | 53.72 | 53.72 | 1 |
| 08/03/90 | 53.50 | 55.72 | (53.45) | 55.45 | 0 |
| 08/06/90 | 54.00 | 57.45 | 54.00 | 57.45 | 0 |
| 08/07/90 | 57.45 | (58.15) | 56.30 | 57.05 | 1 |
| 08/08/90 | 56.75 | 56.90 | 55.05 | 55.05 | 1 |
| 08/09/90 | 54.60 | 54.75 | 53.50 | 53.97 | 1 |

Welcome to the 90's! Commodity price action research has produced several techniques to determine the proximate future of an actively traded commodity option. Questions once thought to have no answer are answered daily: At what price will this swing terminate? . . . Where will this market go after the current swing? . . . How much profit will this option generate tomorrow, . . . this week . . . this month? Swing Analysis attempts to answer such questions with accuracy approaching exactness.

**July 31, 1990** 56.50 57.72 56.20 57.72 0
*Early that night*

$$P_1 = S_a + C - S_1 + (P_f) + (S_f) + (G_f) + (CS_f)$$

$$=- 55.5875 + 57.725 - 53.45 + (54.075 - 57.725) + (55.5875 - 56.20)$$
$$+ [(56.05 - 56.50) + (54.075 - 54.15) + (53.45 - 49.40)$$
$$= 59.125$$

$$P_2 = P_1 + S_a - S_2 + (Pi_f) + [(G\text{-}_f)] + (CS\text{-}_f)$$

$$= 59.125 + 55.5875 - 57.725 + (59.125 - 57.725) + (56.20 - 55.5875)$$
$$+ [(56.20 - 56.05) + (54.15 - 54.075) + (56.20 - 56.50)] + (49.40 - 53.45)$$
$$= 54.2625$$

*Observe that limit down tomorrow is 55.725 basis today's close (57.725). Therefore, the expected low tomorrow is limit down. But limit down (55.725) is lower than today's low (56.20). Consequently, the expected high tomorrow should be a ring high! This market should be sold.*

Suppose tomorrow's high was suspected of being a swing terminus. How could this be verified? Was the 59.125 ring high predicted prior to today's numbers? The answer is yes! Swing Analysis provides the following:

RAE = Ring Average Extension

RAE = Ra + M1 + M2 + (Gf) + (CSf) + Cf)

where Ra = Ring average (last 10 rings)

$M_1$ = Ra - $R_{Boundary}$

M2 = Previous Ring - Previous Ring -2

if Ring = Low then Boundary (1) = Lowest ring in Ra

if Ring = High then Boundary (2) = Highest ring in Ra

Ra = 54.47

RAE = 2x (54.47) - 49.40 + (55.70 - 57.00) + (53.45 - 51.90) + (54.30 - 54.35) + (53.45 - 54.07

= 59.12

*Notice that the Ring low 53.45 was not confirmed until 7/30/90 when the market traded above the previous day's high (54.55). The high 56.05 is higher than the previous ring high (55.72). For this reason the $M_2$ calculation substitutes 56.05 for 55.72.*

Whenever RAE is calculated the result can be "recycled" to yield the next swing target. In this way, the entire next minor swing can be traded. By staying one swing ahead of the market, *perpetual* trading becomes more than a theory. Swing Analysis makes this type of trading possible even though it may not be practical. (It may be more profitable to trade Factor Analysis on a daily basis.)

Suppose weekly price data were collected such that the Open is Monday's open: High equal weekly high; Low equal weekly low and Close equal Friday's close. Applying Swing Analysis to the price data yields powerful position trades. Option traders may find these trades ideal for signaling new transactions. (The same data produces weekly HIGHS and LOWS when Factor Analysis equations are applied.)

The next RAE calculation is as follows:

| | | |
|---|---|---|
| Ra | = | 54.7725 (last nine rings plus 59.12) |
| RAE | = | 2x (54.7725) - 57.00 + (53.45 - 49.40) + (53.45 - 49.40) + (51.90 - 53.45) + (55.725 - 59.125) + (55.725 - 56.20) + (55.725 - 53.45) |
| | = | 53.445 |

The next day's IIigh and Low as well as the next minor swing objective have been analyzed. Based on these calculations the Belly market is headed limit down!

The Factor Analysis trade is:

***SELL A FEB '91 PORK BELLY 58.975. BUY A FEB '91 BELLY 54.40. BUY A FEB '91 BELLY 59.275 STOP!***

The Swing Analysis trade is:

***SELL TWO FEB '91 PORK BELLIES 58.975. BUY A FEB '91 BELLY 59.275 STOP.***

*There is no objective for the Swing Analysis trade because the next broker order will offset this trade and enter a new trade going in the opposite direction. For example, the next trade would be: BUY TWO FEB '91 PORK BELLIES 53.62. SELL A FEB '91 BELLY 53.32 STOP!*

The two trades yield $1,830.00 and $2,140.00 respectively. However, the Swing Analysis trade requires three (3) days while the Factor Analysis trade requires two (2) days. Accordingly, the Factor Analysis trade is more efficient than the Swing Analysis trade. The wise trader would execute both!

**August 1, 1990** 58.60 59.12[1] 55.72[2] 55.72 1
*late evening*

The OPEN and CLOSE represent balancing prices due to the retrostatic effects of the previous and current day's trading. Both are balance prices and, therefore, can be calculated. Trident research revealed a relationship among the OPEN, HIGH, LOW and CLOSE using an interlinking calculation series which independently confirms or validates Factor Analysis $P_1$ and $P_2$. It was believed that the OPEN and CLOSE were completely random occurrences not subject to calculation. However, there appears to be very little about the market that cannot be calculated. The only caution is BE ACCURATE!

The general form of the OPEN equation is:

$$O_c = O + C - O_p + (S_f) + (G_f) + (CS_f) + (C_f)$$

The OPEN calculation for tomorrow's market is:

$$\begin{aligned} O_c &= 58.60 + 55.725 - 57.725 + (56.25 - 56.20) + [(54.15 \\ &\quad - 54.075) + (58.60 - 57.725)] + (55.725 - 59.125) \\ &= 54.20 \end{aligned}$$

The general form of the LOW equation is:

$$L_c = O_c + S_a - S_2 + (G_f) + (S_f) + CS_f)$$

The LOW calculation for tomorrow is:

$L_f$ = 54.20 = 56.25 - 59.125 + [(54.075 - 54.15)] + (55.725 - 53.45)
= 53.525 *(note: this low is beyond limit down (53.72).*

The general form of the HIGH equation is:

$$H_c = L_c + S_a - S_1 + (L_c - O_c) + (G_f)$$

The HIGH calculation for tomorrow is:

$H_c$ = 53.525 + 56.25 - 53.45 + (53.525 - 54.20) + (54.25 - 55.725) + (54.15 - 54.075)
= 54.25

The general form of the CLOSE equation is:

$$C_c = L_c + S_a - H_c + (L - C) + (CS_f)$$

The CLOSE calculation for tomorrow is:

$C_c$ = 53.525 + 56.25 - 54.25 + (54.075 - 54.15) + (55.725 - 55.725) + (0)
= 55.45

Surprise! Surprise! . . . The close calculation indicates a close higher than the high on the day (54.25)! How can this be? Is it a mistake? Or is it another opportunity to make more profit? $770.00 more!

*calculation results:*

| DATE | OPEN | HIGH | LOW | CLOSE |
|---|---|---|---|---|
| 8/02/90 | 54.20 | 54.25 | 53.525 | 55.45 |

The CLOSE calculation is correct. It means that the market should rally after the low (53.525) is reached. But recall the swing target RAE´ (53.475) which was calculated yesterday. The market is certainly entitled to start a new swing after the current swing ends.

> ***SELL A FEB '91 PORK BELLY 54.10 OR BETTER. BUY TWO (2) FEB '91 BELLIES 53.625. BUY A FEB '91 BELLY 54.40 STOP.***

Before this discussion can be concluded another calculation must be made. Recall the predicted ring RAE´ (53.445) from the previous calculation. It is possible to "re-recycle" and get RAE´´. The Swing Analysis calculation is as follows:

$$
\begin{aligned}
R_a'' &= 54.7175 \\
RAE'' &= R_a + M_1 + M_2 + (G_f) + + (CS_f) + (C_f) \\
&= 2x(54.7175) - 49.40 + (53.525 - 53.725) + (55.45 \\
&\quad - 59.125) + (0) + (55.45 - 53.45) \\
&= 58.16
\end{aligned}
$$

This calculation represents the outermost limit of current knowledge. Consider the assumptions involved; (1) the current swing will terminate at 53.445; (2) tomorrow's market will move limit down stopping at 53.725; and (3) the market will open at 53.525 after the limit move; and (4) the market will rally to close at 55.45 after the ring low (53.445).

In practice, an assumption is reinforced after it becomes fact. As soon as a new ring forms another RAE calculation is made. The approach is to replace assumption with fact. By doing this a Trader can stay at least one swing ahead of the market.

The years since Trident Strategy have been very fruitful. Research resulted in a variety of specialized technical tools which answer most of the practical questions with regard to a particular trade. The market's own mechanics have been tapped with a view toward maximizing profit opportunity. Strategy has given way to common sense. If you know what the market must do, doesn't common sense require you to take advantage of that knowledge?

## TRADING PERSPECTIVE

It is not expected that the reader can now successfully apply Factor Analysis or Retrostasis. These new developments are shown only as examples of what is now possible using the basic Trident ideas.

Trident on its own is a valuable, highly profitable tool.